Mary Cassatt

Mary Cassatt

by

JULIA M. H. CARSON

Illustrated with photographs
from paintings and color prints
by MARY CASSATT

DAVID McKAY COMPANY, INC.

New York

1966

MARY CASSATT

Library of Congress Catalog Card Number: 66-10780

MANUFACTURED IN THE UNITED STATES OF AMERICA

VAN REES PRESS • NEW YORK

Grateful acknowledgment is made for permission to quote from the following:

Degas et Son Oeuvre, by P. A. Lemoisne, vol. 1, 1946. Reprinted by permission of Arts et
Métiers, Graphique, Paris.

Degas Letters, tr. by Marguerite Kay, ed. by Marcel Guerin, 1947. Reprinted by permission
of Bruno Cassirer Ltd., Oxford.

Recollections of a Picture Dealer, by Ambroise Vollard, 1936. Reprinted by permission of
Constable and Company, Ltd., London.

"Letters from Mary Cassatt to Durand-Ruel," *Les Archives de l'Impressionisme*, by Lionel
Venturi, vol. 2, 1939. Reprinted by permission of Charles Durand-Ruel, Paris.

Renoir, My Father, copyright 1958, 1962, by Jean Renoir. Reprinted by permission of Little,
Brown and Company, Boston.

Dictionary of Modern Painting, ed. by Carlton Lake and Robert Maillard, Paris, Fernand
Hazan, 1953. Reprinted by permission of Paris Book Center, Inc., New York.

Letters to His Son Lucien, by Camille Pissarro. Copyright 1943 by Pantheon Books, Inc. Reprinted by permission of Random House, Inc., New York.

Correspondance de Berthe Morisot, by Denis Rouart, Quatre Chemins-Editart, Paris, 1950.
Reprinted by permission of Denis Rouart.

Graphic Work of Mary Cassatt, a Catalogue Raisonné, by Adelyn D. Breeskin. New York,
Bittner, 1948. Reprinted by permission of Mrs. Breeskin.

Impressionist Painting in the Louvre, by Germain Bazin. Reprinted by permission of Thames
and Hudson, Ltd., London and Harry N. Abrams, New York.

French XVIII Century Painters, by Edmond and Jules de Goncourt. Tr. by Robin Ironside,
1948. Reprinted by permission of the Phaidon Press Ltd., London.

Masterpieces of European Painting in America, ed. by Hans Tietze, 1939. Reprinted by permission of Oxford University Press, New York.

Edgar Degas, by Pierre Cabanne. Paris; Editions Pierre Tisné, 1958. Reprinted by permission
of Laurent Tisné.

History of Impressionism, by John Rewald. New York, The Museum of Modern Art, 1961.
Reprinted by permission of John Rewald.

Mary Cassatt, by Forbes Watson. American Artists Series, 1932. Reprinted by permission of
the Whitney Museum of American Art, New York.

To my sister

Catharine L. Hicks

ACKNOWLEDGMENTS

I want to acknowledge first of all my great indebtedness to Mary Cassatt's family: Mrs. Horace Binney Hare (Ellen Mary Cassatt, the painter's niece), Mrs. John B. Thayer (Lois B. Cassatt, the painter's great-niece), and Mr. and Mrs. Alexander J. Cassatt (the painter's great-nephew and his wife). They have given me every possible assistance through loaning me letters, writing letters of introduction for me and sharing their own recollections of the artist and the facts they have been told about her. No family could have been more cooperative. I am grateful for their permission to quote from their documents.

To the American Philosophical Society I owe the opportunity to do research in Paris, especially at the Bibliothèque Nationale and in the Durand-Ruel library; to visit Mary Cassatt's chateau, Beaufresne, near Beauvais; and to study in Parma, Italy. Their grant was from the Penrose Fund.

To the Havemeyers and to the Metropolitan Museum of New York I owe permission to quote extensively from Mrs. H. O. Havemeyer's privately printed *Sixteen to Sixty, Memoirs of a Collector*. No other source except the letters gives so vivid a picture of Mary Cassatt in action.

The staff of the New York Public Library were at all times helpful and resourceful, especially those in the Print Room and in the Art and Architecture Division. My special thanks go to Miss Naomi Street. I am particularly grateful also for permission to use for three months The Wertheim Study.

The personnel at the Bibliothèque Nationale were imaginative and untiring in their aid. I greatly appreciate their assistance.

The Archives of American Art in Detroit were of substantial help in permitting use of their microfilm material on Mary Cassatt. I want to thank especially Mr. Garnett McCoy.

Picture credits are given with the reproductions and the gratitude of the publisher and myself goes to those who have so graciously permitted their use. In this connection I wish to thank especially M. Charles Durand-Ruel for his most generous help in securing for me prints of many of Mary Cassatt's pictures formerly or currently in his possession. To his kindness in permitting the use of the Gallery's library I am indebted for valuable material.

Thanks are due also to Mr. J. Howard Whittemore and to Mr. Donald W. Pierpont, and others for permission to quote from letters.

Grateful acknowledgment is made for permission to quote from the documents on pages 177-186.

To Bertha L. Gunterman, my editor, I owe a special debt for her continuing and inspiring interest in this project and for her meticulous editorial work.

To my husband I am tremendously grateful for happy and enlightening companionship in this exploration.

                                                                    J.M.H.C.

CONTENTS

ILLUSTRATIONS

Chapter I

TOWARD THE PARIS SALON

One day when she was scarcely more than twenty, Mary Cassatt told her father she wanted to be a professional painter.

Neither the time nor the place — nor the father — was auspicious for such an announcement. It was the second half of the nineteenth century, and ladies in comfortable circumstances were expected to be decorative in an inconspicuous way and at leisure. "Professional" meant earning money. No Cassatt woman had ever done such a thing. As for being an artist — words failed the family, except for Mary's mother, who was inclined to be sympathetic.

It was true that Philadelphians were proud of their family portraits. It was proper to have them on the walls, though the owner's pride was in the likeness rather than in the execution. Little art intruded and was of interest to no one. Painting was not an occupation that even a man — a sensible, practical man — would consider as a life work. For a young woman of good breeding, the idea was preposterous.

Added to the negative atmosphere of time and place was her father's position. Mr. Cassatt was a respected, conservative banker. He was also the authoritative head of his family, not a stern man but just and extremely dignified. Of all this Mary

1

was aware when she entered his presence to lay her proposal before him. She had expected her decision would be a shock to him even though it was he who had taken the family to museums and galleries abroad. But she had not anticipated such consternation as she now saw in his face. For a moment her blue-gray eyes wavered. But they soon steadied. She had stated her decision and would bide her time. She had been a long while making up her own mind about being a professional artist. It was fair that her father, too, should take his time. Perhaps he had never before stopped to think that fine paintings were not impersonally manufactured but were created by people who loved color and form and design as she did.

Later on in France when Mary spoke vigorously about her native country — "I am an American, definitely and frankly American"[1] — she meant every word of it. She meant also that she was a Philadelphia Cassatt. Being a Cassatt gave her status that she took for granted. She did not exploit it. There was no need. Society was there for her whenever she wanted it. It was second nature for her to move among people at the top. It gave her fearlessness. There was not a trace of braggadocio about Mary Cassatt. But she expected respect and good manners.

She was accustomed to being with people who succeeded. Her father was a successful financier, her mother a woman of broad culture. Their friends were building impressive lives in business or in society. Being a sensible person, not very introspective, she pursued her life with the sureness of one who assumes that success follows due effort. Though there was arrogance in her, it was never in regard to what she did herself. That she was arrogant in her dedication to art was true enough. She was capable of scorching rebuke to fellow painters who slumped below their own capacities. And she could be bitingly intolerant of stupid people who said stupid things about painting. Annoyed with Sargent for the painting he made of her brother, she told Aleck he ought not to have the thing in his house; and when Sargent called on her in Paris afterward she was not at home to him. This was less personal animus than the conviction that he had painted her brother less well than he could have done.

For success in the family enterprises there was need for aggressiveness and independent judgment. Mary Cassatt came naturally by her intrepidity. Also she shared her family's practical acumen. She had wealth, but she managed her money carefully. And with it all went a certain pioneering spirit, a true American resourcefulness. Like her brother Aleck, who was to be president of the Pennsylvania Railroad, it never occurred to her not to do things herself if that seemed at the time the best way to get them done. As a young railroad official, Aleck sometimes drove a locomotive himself — and hugely enjoyed it. And his sister, experimenting with color prints in her later life, did not hesitate to run her own press.

The family conservatism, then, was relative to the times, and in no way hindered the independence and scope of her work. In her social world, however, Old Philadelphia set the tone and decreed an impeccable course. She cared little for society as such, but friends of her own choosing were essential to her. Some of them were in the social register. Not all. Her · hospitality and graciousness were recognized by people of various interests and backgrounds. But a certain punctiliousness as well as good breeding governed her social life.

She was proud of her ancestry. In a history written for the family by her grandmother is the following: "The Cassats [sic] were originally French — they were Huguenots, and at the time of the dreadful persecutions of that sect, fled to Holland. They were three brothers. Afterward one apostatized, went back to France and inherited their estates.* Their French name was Cazar; ** in Holland it was Cassart. They married in Holland, Holland wives. They came to America and first settled in New Jersey and thence in 1760 came to what was then York County, that part which is now Adams County [Pennsylvania] — forty years before the division — and settled on the property on which their descendants still live [1888]."

Probably apocryphal was Mr. Cassatt's reply to his daughter when she told him she wished to be a painter: "I would almost rather see you dead." Nothing in his subsequent relationship with her justifies such an extreme remark. At any rate, the severity of his first reaction was presently lessened by his own views on education. "Our father," Mary said later, "did not have at all the soul of a businessman," and "He devoted himself to our education." [2] But Mr. Cassatt had to be sure his young daughter was in earnest. If she really wanted artistic training, the proposal might conceivably be considered. There was no hurry. And there were questions to be asked: Wasn't she enjoying her life — her frequent trips abroad with members of the family; her long, leisurely visits to friends and relatives; the tennis and boating parties, the horseback riding; evenings at the theatre and opera?

Of course she enjoyed all these. She would hope to go on enjoying some of them, but as recreation, not as the main

* *Mary Cassatt's niece, Mrs. Horace Binney Hare, doubted the accuracy of this sentence. She wrote: "My Aunt was never able to find any records of Cassarts in France."*
** *Mary Cassatt's great-nephew, Alexander J. Cassatt, corrects this to Cossart.*

business of living. She wanted to make something more substantial of her life, to live as an individual person. She wanted to become a painter, a professional.

Not long after their initial interview, her father suggested that Mary study at the Pennsylvania Academy of the Fine Arts. It was the oldest art school in the country. Mary hesitated hardly at all. She knew even then that this was not what she wanted, that she could not learn to be an artist from didactic teaching. The only way for her would be first-hand study of the great masters with a chance to learn through copying their paintings. Of great masters there were none at the Pennsylvania Academy. Still she was wise in the ways of her family, even in her early twenties, and she agreed to go. The experience proved even more dismal than she had expected. "There was no instruction," she said later. "I knew moreover that painting was not taught. . . . The teaching of museums suffices." [3]

Such museums as then existed in America were far from adequate. Though there were in private collections a few good paintings, America had not yet developed a compelling desire for the fine arts. The first American museum, founded in Philadelphia by Charles Willson Peale, was started in 1785, "with the skeleton of a mastodon which had just been unearthed, and later assembled in one room Peale's portraits of celebrated Americans and a collection of stuffed birds." [4] An early devotee of art, James Jackson Jarves, had done his vigorous best to awaken the country to its artistic poverty. Among other things he had brought back from Europe a discriminating collection of Italian primitives, which were exhibited upon two occasions in the 1860's. He was unable to find a permanent home for them until he deposited them at Yale as security for a loan. When he was unable to repay the loan, they were put up at auction, but no bidders appeared. "So that Yale University, almost against its will, became the owner of a collection which is now regarded as a treasure-house of early Italian art." [5]

America's absorption in her economic development was in part responsible for her early indifference to the arts. Another factor was the puritanical attitude widely prevalent. "Men are not pleased with the figure they make in their own imaginations," Emerson had written, "and they flee to art and convey their better sense in an oratorio, a statue or a picture. Art makes the same effort which a sensual prosperity makes, namely to detach the beautiful from the useful, to do up the work as unavoidable and, hating it, pass on to enjoyment. These solaces and compensations, this division of beauty from use, the laws of nature do not permit. As soon as beauty is sought, not from religion and love, but from pleasure, it degrades the seeker."

For a brief period Mary Cassatt drew dutifully from casts at the Pennsylvania Academy and copied paintings scarcely worth their frames. Then abruptly she decided to stop wasting time. She must go abroad to work. She would stay with friends in France. To her father it seemed a reasonable request to visit family friends, and there was no harm in her looking at paintings in museums during her spare time.

She stayed three years abroad, mostly in France. As early as 1869 she was writing home about "we professionals" in contrast to amateur painters. This could only mean that she was acquiring a professional point of view toward the world of art she had chosen. Not yet had she produced work of her own to justify the term. Then to avoid the Franco-Prussian War she returned to Philadelphia. But in 1872 she sailed for Italy, with Parma her destination.

The color of Parma delighted her — the orange-red tile roofs, the black-green cypresses, the warm creams and light browns of the buildings. Behind wrought-iron gates touched with gilt, courtyards blazed with great salmon-colored urns of bright geraniums. In the fall, purple grapes hung heavy against leaves slipping into gold. There was gold again in the ceilings and frescoes of Correggio and in the work of Parmigianino; a golden haze seemed, in fact, to envelop the buildings of the city and to soften the brilliance of the painting.

There was so much to be seen that Mary Cassatt walked and walked, seeking wherever possible the large red paving stones, so much easier on the feet than the cobbled streets. At the corner of the Strada al Duomo she often went up the grayish-pink steps of the eight-sided Baptistery, reputed to be the finest romanesque monument in northern Italy, its exterior palest salmon and gray with bronze doors.

Working at the Parma academy with the painter and engraver Carlo Raimondi, she still managed to spend long hours in the eleventh-century Duomo, elegantly romanesque, where Correggio's frescoes of the Assumption decorate the dome high above the elaborate gold-colored chandeliers and the great pillars of reddish-amber marble. Less neck-breaking was the lower Camera di S. Paolo, also the work of Correggio. The vault was dark green with ropes of dull gold decorated with medallions — exquisite paintings of children and animals.

In Parma, as elsewhere, Mary Cassatt was interested in other arts. After dinner in the evenings there was the Teatro Regio, built by the music lovers of Parma to honor Verdi, and the seventeenth-century Farnese Theatre on the top floor of the

Palazzo della Pilotta made entirely of wood. If the steep banks
of theatre seats were a little difficult to negotiate in the long
and elaborate gowns of the period, the view she had of the
stage, once she was seated, was magnificent.

If she missed too much the bridle paths around Philadelphia, she could canter over the nearby countryside that had
its own charm. The flowers were much the same as at home,
the apple trees and pears more severely pruned. In the autumn,
the corn ripening in the fields looked like Pennsylvania corn,
though not nearly as tall. Or was she gazing at it with homesick eyes? But she was sure about the trees — theirs back home
would overshadow all she could see as she turned in her saddle
surveying the terrain. There were no silvery olives as far north
as this. What trees there were had whitish trunks free halfway
up of leaves and branches. Lovely pictures some of them made.
She pulled her mare to a standstill to enjoy the fine S-bend of
a stream lined with high-trimmed poplars.

But it was, most of all, Parma's art that set her enthusiasm
aflame. "For eight months," she said later, "I went to school
to Correggio — a prodigious Master!" [6] Among other things
Correggio's children impressed her. There was no confusing
these flesh-and-blood babies with conventional putti. Nor were
they small-sized adults. High overhead in the vault of the
Camera di S. Paolo she gazed at a youngster hugging the neck
of a dog nearly as large as himself. The roll of the dog's eye,
half-fearful of being choked, yet pleased with affection — both
of these young animals were certainly alive.

For the actual business of copying, Correggio's pictures in
frames were more satisfactory than the somewhat distant frescoes. She delighted in the laughing angel in the *Madonna of
St. Jerome*. What a wealth of Correggio there was in Parma!
Nor did she overlook the Parmigianinos or El Greco's *Healing*

of the Blind Man, Holbein's *Portrait of Erasme* or the beautiful head of a young girl by Leonardo da Vinci. But it was under the influence of Correggio that she painted *On the Balcony* (The Philadelphia Museum of Art). Later a critic said of this painting, "disclosing two alluring majas with an ardent majo standing behind . . . . Miss Cassatt's work of this period was strikingly competent and disclosed not inconsiderable sensuous charm." [7] Signing the canvas with her first two names, Mary Stevenson, but omitting the Cassatt, she submitted it to the Paris Salon. To her great delight it was accepted.

Her family, now somewhat more reconciled to her odd interest in art, observed her progress. From Altoona, Pennsylvania, her brother, Aleck, wrote to the girl * who was to be his wife: "I received a letter from Mary the other day. She is in high spirits as her picture has been accepted for the annual exhibition in Paris. This you must understand is a great honor for a young artist and not only has it been accepted but it has been hung on the 'line.' I don't know exactly what that means myself but suppose it means that it has been hung in a favorable position. Mary's art name is 'Mary Stevenson' under which name I suppose she expects to become famous, poor child."

From Parma she went to Spain. "The Rubens of the Prado Museum excited me with such admiration," she said later, "that I ran from Madrid to Antwerp. I remained there all one summer to study Rubens." [8] The following year (1873) the

---

* *Lois Buchanan, niece of President Buchanan. The Alexander J. Cassatts were to have four children: Edward Buchanan Cassatt ("Eddie") whose daughter is now Mrs. John B. Thayer; Katharine; Elsie; and Robert Kelso Cassatt whose wife was Minnie Drexel Fell and whose sons are Alexander J. Cassatt and Anthony Cassatt.*

Salon accepted a second painting — a picture of a torero to whom a young girl offers a glass of water.

While she was staying in Paris in 1873 she had an experience similar to the impact of Correggio and of Rubens. "How well I remember . . . seeing for the first time Degas' pastels in the window of a picture dealer on the Boulevard Haussmann," she later wrote to Mrs. Havemeyer. "I used to go and flatten my nose against that window and absorb all I could of his art. It changed my life. I saw art then as I wanted to see it." [9]

Working in Rome the next winter, she painted the head of a girl with hair that was "almost red." She said it was done under the influence of Rubens.[10] Perhaps there was another influence also. This painting, the third to be accepted by the Salon, showed in contrast to its predecessors a new force at work. Something had liberated fresh possibilities in Mary Cassatt. She had found a more congenial approach, possibly revealed to her while her nose was flattened against the window where Degas' work was on display.

Degas' brilliant originality was already leading him into new approaches to painting. For nearly a decade he had exhibited at the Salon, but now he was moving toward greater independence and away from any connection with the official art world that he felt was stifling creativity. All his life an ardent admirer of Ingres, he held himself to the highest standards of draftsmanship, no matter how far and wide his imagination soared.

Mary Cassatt was not to meet Degas for several years after her 1874 showing of the red-haired girl. Nor was she aware at the time of this exhibition that Degas had said to a friend, as they stood admiring this painting of hers, "There is someone who feels as I do." [11]

With three pictures accepted for exhibition by the Salon

over a three-year period, Mary decided to settle in Paris. Soon her tall, slim figure became a familiar sight in her neighborhood and in the Louvre. "She favored, when en promenade, sober-toned, often russet-brown pleated frocks with white frills at wrists and neck, and carried a parasol with an air . . . ." [12] Her French was fluent, for Mrs. Cassatt had insisted her children speak it from the time they were youngsters. And yet for all the years she was to spend in France she never acquired what her great-niece called "a pretty accent." There is a tale that Renoir met her on one of his painting trips in Brittany and enjoyed talking to her. According to his son, Jean, she said to Renoir one day: "I adore the brown tones in your shadows. Tell me how you do it."

"When you pronounce your *r's*," he replied. [13]

Mary had lived in Paris before, but her home had then been elsewhere. Now she established herself with a feeling of permanence. She retained, however, some of the habits she had grown accustomed to in America. One was riding. She stabled her horse near the Bois de Boulougne and rode whenever she could find the time. Paris suited both her basic serenity and her vigor. It kept life in balance as she worked hard to improve her art and, at the same time, continued alert to what was going on around her. Many young painters were copying in the Louvre. As she set up her easel, she felt part of the pulse of Paris. In this beautiful city the seriousness, the importance of art were not questioned. None of your energy need be spent making a case for the painter. Coming from Philadelphia, rather arid then in the arts, Mary found this different atmosphere at once restful and stimulating.

She liked, too, the savoring of daily living that was part of the city's charm. People made an art of the way they went through their usual routine. They were alive in the moment and enjoyed it. The moment might include almost anything: the fine weather, a satisfying luncheon leisurely consumed, a heartfelt, short-lived outburst at a vehicle careless of pedestrians, and then the calm beauty of the broad streets and the stately white houses with their close black-iron balconies. If Parisians were publicly more demonstrative than Americans, Mary recognized the genuineness of the impulse and respected the strength of the feeling. She was quite aware that what a person felt was the mainspring of art.

Soon she fell into the habit of strolling about the city. She liked the extent of the formal parks and gardens, the naturalness of the woods. The intrinsic smartness of the people was congenial to her own sense of style. Though she painted long hours, she found in Paris a lack of the hurried pressures that had sometimes troubled her in Philadelphia. Common sense told her that drive for its own sake was an enemy of creative work. There must be pauses for brooding over what one was feeling.

Before long she recognized that what she was feeling had changed. She was not now quite the same person who had painted the torero. What did she know about bullfighters? Not a thing. But about other sorts of people she did know. Able critics were later to speak of the psychological penetration in Mary Cassatt's best work. Little evidence exists that she turned an analytical eye upon herself as a person. Rather, she was totally absorbed by what she saw, by what she perceived outside herself. There was objectivity in her straight look. But all the while she seems to have kept deep within her an area of serenity where she did not permit disturbance.

The city to which she had come from temporary residence in Rome had had several years to recover from the Siege of Paris. A feeling of transition was in the air, touched with the exhilaration of new freedom. Politically, socially, and in the arts, channelled ways of proceeding had been disrupted. Gone was exclusive aristocratic patronage of the arts. The rising men of wealth came largely from a middle class that coveted art as a means of increasing their own importance. Their demand was therefore for the painting and sculpture that royalty and court circles had accepted and patronized over the years. But so-called official art had fallen for the most part into the hands of men who looked to the past and were indifferent or aggressively opposed to innovation. Virility and genuine creative impulse were infrequent among those in the high posts of official French art. It was these men, some of them skilled technicians, who controlled the Salon and presided over the training of novices. At the urging of her family, Mary herself had worked briefly — very briefly — in the fashionable atelier of one of them — Charles Chaplin.

But now with a new sense of personal independence permeating French life, certain artists were vigorously questioning the old forms and procedures. Here and there an individual free spirit had soared to life in Paris, drawing strength from intense interest in contemporary life. As artists these painters were not preoccupied with classical periods, with mythology or with formalized portrayal of religious subjects. They had ceased to look backward and had turned to explore their immediate surroundings, both as subject-matter and as challenge for the development of new methods. It was the essence of all this that had come through the windowpane to Mary Cassatt as she had gazed at Degas' work.

For the next Salon (1875) Mary painted a full-length portrait of her sister Lydia against a light background. To her surprise and dismay it was refused. When she had recovered from the initial shock and was able to view the situation dispassionately, she began to suspect the reason for the rejection. Salon portraits customarily had somber backgrounds. Acting upon her suspicion, she repainted the background, darkening it, and again submitted the canvas the following year. It was accepted. Her disillusionment with Salon standards brought a curl to her lip and a strong surge of distaste. Still she would be fair. She would try again. But her next submission was refused.

This was the year (1877) that her father, mother, and her sister Lydia arrived to make Paris their permanent home. This move left in Pennsylvania, of their immediate family, only her two brothers, Aleck and Gardner.* Comfortable living quarters were found for Mary and her family at 12 avenue Trudaine, and she had her studio at 6 Boulevard Clichy.

Meanwhile she was witnessing the neglect or abuse that both public and critics were giving the work of Manet, Pissarro, Renoir, Degas and their friends. One of the few constructive comments was made by Georges Rivière in the spring when he wrote: "Monsieur Degas: How can I talk aptly about this essentially Parisian artist who displays in each of his works as much literary and philosophical talent as linear art and knowledge of color? With one line he says better and more quickly all that can be said about him, because his works are always witty, refined and sincere. He does not try to make us credit a naïveté which he cannot possess; on the contrary his prodigious science is blaring everywhere; his ingenuousness, so attractive and so particular in its kind, places the figures in the most unpredictable and amusing fashion which at the same time [is] always true and always normal. Indeed, what Monsieur Degas despises above all is romantic dizziness, the sub-

---

* A third brother, Robert Kelso Cassatt, had died in Germany at the age of twelve and been buried at Darmstadt.

At the Milliner's, by Degas. (Mary Cassatt posed for this.)

stitution of dreams of life, in a word: magniloquence...." [14]
With such remarks Mary Cassatt was in accord. Dreams of
life were not for her. She was too normal, too much alive in
the world as it was.

It gratified her to learn that Degas had observed other work
of hers and that he wanted Tourny, the etcher, whom she had
met while studying Rubens in Antwerp, to take him to her
studio. When this introduction took place, Degas was "enchanted with what she showed him." [15]

What Mary herself saw when he was presented to her was
a neatly dressed man in his early forties with brilliant eyes, a
determined jaw and a mouth that in repose was sullen. In fact
when his concentrated gaze was bent on her work the set of
his face was dour and forbidding. Observing him thus she
could easily credit the tales she had heard of his cruel wit and
sardonic criticism. But when he turned to look at her and
smiled, she saw a totally different man — kind and generous
and — Was it shy? For a moment she had a fleeting glimpse of
a sensitive person usually protected by a truculent facade. Ah
well, she had encountered facades before. It was the artist
behind the mask whose praise and judgment she valued.

"Degas," she said later, "persuaded me not to send my work
to the Salon any longer and to show with his friends in the
group of Impressionists. I accepted with joy. Finally I could
work with absolute independence without concern for the
eventual opinion of a jury. Already I had recognized those
who were my true masters. I admired Manet, Courbet and
Degas. I detested conventional art. I began to live." [16]

I detested conventional art — Strange words from the daughter of a Philadelphia banker in the last quarter of the nineteenth century? Or was this further evidence of the same di-

chotomy that had caused her to leave her family for the wider world of professional art while scrupulously maintaining in her non-professional life the strict standards and habits of her up-bringing? At any rate the implications of her alignment with Degas and his friends, together with the continuing propriety of her social and behavioral values, revealed a pattern that was to govern her life. Charm, graciousness and lively, intelligent conversation attracted well-known people to her home: the statesman Clemenceau, the poet Mallarmé, the writer George Moore and other eminent people, as well as her paint-ing colleagues. Relatives and friends from America were also frequent visitors. Her guests found a household beautifully managed. Immaculately uniformed servants insured comfort and ease. The dresses of the hostess were from fine dressmakers in Paris.

In contrast was her working life. Here, like Degas, Mary Cassatt did not always have time for the amenities. Or the in-clination. The courtesy of her social life evaporated if anyone cast aspersions upon art. Her tongue was sharp and unbridled when a painter prostituted his abilities. Wrote Forbes Wat-son, formerly of the Whitney Museum of American Art: "She had to the end a sense of elegance that encompassed both her art and her living. Yet from no lips have I heard less ingratiat-ing language when her passionately-held artistic beliefs were threatened. The elegance that was Mary Cassatt's had its lim-itations. This was due to a fierce love of truth which made it impossible for her to say a gracious word to the conniving or to flatter the painter who had been untrue to himself. Miss Cassatt sent more than one inelegant message to those of her contemporaries who allowed their gifts to become tainted by worldliness. And upon stupid visitors who came to see her from idle curiosity, she could exercise a bitter tongue . . . . Art

was her life. She hated all who thought of it softly and sen-
timentally." [17]

Perhaps this was not too surprising. Mary Cassatt was thoroughly American, and America in the third quarter of the
nineteenth century, when she was growing up, was still, in
some of its activities and attitudes, a pioneering country. Philadelphia gentlemen, so courteous and considerate socially, were
— like others of their fellow-countrymen — establishing posi-
tions as captains of industry, as resourceful business and professional men. It was often a rigorous proceeding. During
working hours they spoke their minds and imposed their wills.
If from them came Mary's business acumen, from them she
also learned to scorn anything substandard. She left no one in
doubt as to her convictions — and prejudices. Even to the
irascible, charming, dedicated but cynical Degas she stood up
vigorously when occasion demanded it. Mrs. Havemeyer once
said: ". . . Degas was addicted to the habit of throwing verbal
vitriol, as the French call it, upon his friends and Miss Cassatt
would not have been the daughter of the Cassatts if she had
not been equal to parrying his thrusts . . . ." [18]

Meanwhile who were for her the dramatis personae when
she made her home in Paris? Though Courbet was no longer
living there, she felt his influence. Throughout his vigorous
life he had worked to clear a new road. Banishing gods, goddesses, sentimental conceptions and formalized religious subjects, he had firmly knocked on the head the decadent schools
of both classical and romantic painting. With much talk and
prolific work he had established Nature and contemporary
people as possible subjects for art — provided the artist used
his eyes and put on canvas exactly what he saw. Courbet
painted what he knew first-hand: stone-breakers, peasants,
nudes, rocks, fields, animals, trees. Mary became deeply im-

bued with the realism he so insistently brought to the fore. She responded wholeheartedly to being an artist of her own time. Her disposition would have been antipathetic to Courbet in the flesh. The burly son of a prosperous landowner with a good deal of the peasant in him, Courbet's conceit was enormous and his exhibitionism formidable on occasion. But Mary Cassatt's steady eye, her objectivity, her analytical mind and the forthright sincerity of her feelings made her appreciative of all he had contributed toward the acceptance of contemporary subject-matter. She admired his adamant adherence to truth as he saw it.

Achille Segard says she felt she must be of her time. "She understood that all the great painters, in order to become artists for all time, had been first interpreters of their epoch . . . ." He adds, "Mary Cassatt's sympathetic movement toward the group of rejected artists involved nothing of sentimentality. Before becoming devoted to their work, she had not known any of these artists. By the chance of her visits to exhibitions she had discovered them. Her eyes, already well trained, had discerned what there was in them of originality and excellence. She felt with them an affinity of taste and sensibility. It was by a voluntary personal act, by spontaneous choice, by a decision of the spirit that she had promised to follow their efforts with energy and to work *dans le même sens*. It was by an act of free judgment that she had separated them, in her mind, from the ordinary production of the painters of that epoch." With enthusiasm he continues: "Such incisiveness of opinion, such decision in her choice of her intellectual masters, a taste so sure and a fearlessness so young, so generous in the affirmation of her preferences would have been worthy of being noted in the history of the beginnings of any artist. In the case of a young girl, a stranger, relatively isolated in Paris and living

in a milieu where it would be natural that one would have
respect for consecrated reputations, the situation takes on, in
my eyes, a value of great import. These are traits of character
that reveal to us a remarkable personality." [19]

Though Courbet had left the city two years before Mary
Cassatt settled there, three painters who continued to work in
or near Paris were to be important to her: Manet, Pissarro and
Degas. Manet was a dozen years her senior. She saw less of
him than of his work. To his work she gave concentrated
study. He had not only taken advantage of the road Courbet
and his predecessors had cleared of outworn subjects and conceptions, but he moved along it with new techniques. Mary
observed these developments with close attention. What was
there here she could learn that would strengthen her own way
of seeing and its interpretation on canvas?

Manet had courage, too, which she admired. Courage and
a touch of naïveté. Should he not have foreseen, for instance,
the outcry when he painted his *Le Déjeuner sur l'Herbe*
(1863), somewhat like a picture by Giorgione and an engraving after Raphael,[20] clothing the men in modern dress, lightly
draping one woman, painting the other nude? Given the then
state of French art and the predispositions of critics and public, he should not have been surprised that he was violently
attacked. There were blind spots in Manet as well as genius.
It was his personal tragedy that he coveted acceptance by the
highest official circles in the world of art, that he longed for
Salon recognition and to be a Chevalier of the Legion of
Honor. Fortunately his genuine ability, his inner compulsion
toward the truth as he saw it, blocked for a long while the
achievement he thought he wanted. More recently (1873),
Mary knew, there had been *Le Bon Bock*, a portrait of the
engraver Bellot at the Café Guerbois. It was Manet's first

public success in a dozen years, and how hugely he enjoyed it! Accepted by the Salon, it was promptly purchased by Faure, the singer. But some of Manet's fellow-painters missed in *Le Bon Bock* what they considered most excellent in his usual work. Mary Cassatt was among them.

Still, on the whole, she had great admiration for Manet and was to be instrumental in enriching America with many of his best pictures. He could not but have felt her friendliness and the value of her dispassionate judgment. They had long talks occasionally, as when he came back from Italy soon after she settled in Paris. "Manet told me," she later said to Mrs. Havemeyer, "that he had been a long time in Venice. I believe he spent the winter there and he was thoroughly discouraged and depressed at his inability to paint anything to his satisfaction. He had just decided to give it up and return home to Paris. On his last afternoon in Venice, he took a fairly small canvas and went out on the Grand Canal just to make a sketch to recall his visit. He told me he was so pleased with the result of his afternoon's work that he decided to remain over a day and finish it." [21] The painting was his *Blue Venice*.

George Moore, another of Mary's friends, was also an admirer of Manet. Moore was an Irishman in his twenties who had come to Paris to study painting under the academician Cabanel. After a time he abandoned painting for writing. Manet's pastel of him in the New York Metropolitan Museum of Art shows a long, thin face with rough beard running up to his unruly hair. His expression is not as alert as his writing revealed him to be. Fascinated by the group of artists he met at the Nouvelle Athènes in Paris, he wrote vividly about them. The Nouvelle Athènes was a café on the Place Pigalle where Manet and Degas were regular patrons. A couple of tables were always reserved for them and their friends, who included not only artists but a few critics and writers. The café's painted ceiling featured the portrait of a large dead rat, and the unconventional atmosphere in general did not make the Nouvelle Athènes in the 1870's a place that a woman of Mary's upbringing would patronize. "But," wrote Moore, "she lived on the Boulevard Extérieur, her studio was within a minute's walk of the Place Pigalle and we used to see her every day." Perhaps to her he made the remark, partial to Manet, that he later committed to print: "Manet was an instinct, Degas an intellectuality." He amplified the way this difference impressed him: *"The Mona Lisa* and Degas' *Leçon de Danse* are intellectual pictures, they were painted with the brains rather than with the temperaments; and what is any intellect compared to a gift like Manet's?" [22] But Moore enjoyed talking to Degas. One day he told Degas he did not care for Daumier. Degas replied, "If you were to show Raphael a Daumier he would admire it, he would take off his hat; but if you were to show him a Cabanel he would say with a sigh, 'That is my fault.' " [23]

Pissarro, older than the others, was a friend to all the Impressionists. With a large family to support, and little sale for his paintings, he led a tormented life — except when he was before his easel. The most generous of counselors to his fellow painters, no technique he developed was kept secret from them. At one time or another, several of them set their easels beside his and painted the same scene. Mary did so when, one summer, they lived next each other in the country. Though she had little interest in landscape painting, as far as her own work was concerned, since she was to do figures with rarely a touch of view behind them, she admired Pissarro greatly both as painter and teacher. "He was so much a teacher," she said, "that he could have taught stones how to draw correctly." [24] To his younger contemporaries he may have given much the same advice he gave his painter sons: "Scorn my judgment. I have such a longing for you all to be great that I cannot hide my opinions from you. Accept only those that are in accord with your sentiments and mode of understanding . . . . Be bold, then, and to work!" [25] It was advice suited to Mary Cassatt's nature. Never a copyist, she took for herself only what would improve her work.

This was true even with Degas — Degas the artist and the man who had so much in common with her: conventional parents in comfortable circumstances, a father who had to be persuaded to let his son abandon the study of law for art, sincerity and devotion to what he believed true in painting, an independence as proud and forceful as her own. Largely impervious to the judgment of their colleagues, they were both to work exactly as they pleased — he a bachelor ten years her senior, she apparently without thought of marriage. Never was he her teacher in a formal sense, though often her adviser. On her side, she had opinions about his work which she sometimes expressed, and when he could not make a model understand the pose he wanted, she occasionally offered to pose herself, as in his millinery series.

But of supreme importance was her belief in what Degas stood for. "In Degas she recognized and admired one of the great classical masters of French painting . . . . The ease and supreme sureness of his rigorous design aroused her great admiration. She observed the originality of feeling, the exactitude of movement seized at a characteristic moment, the refinement of his visual sensibility. Certain harmonies of tones, almost acid, gave her the feeling of green fruit in the mouth; other harmonies seemed mellow and dissolving as if a sort of tenderness, very noble and very intellectual, had been

crushed under the thumb at the same time as the colored
crayon." [26]

There were others in her early Paris life. Among her acquaintances were Marie Bracquemond, who with her husband
showed work in the fourth and fifth Impressionist Exhibitions,
and Eva Gonzalès, Manet's only pupil. Previously Eva had
studied with the fashionable Chaplin, in whose studio Mary
had worked for a short while. There is an account of Manet's
method of teaching Eva Gonzalès that suggests the approach
of some of the artists who were Mary Cassatt's contemporaries.
Manet would "arrange some grapes on the corner of a white
tablecloth, a slice of salmon on a silver platter, as well as a
knife, and say, 'Do this quickly! Don't pay too much attention
to the background. Preoccupy yourself mostly with the values.
Do you understand? When you look at this [still life], and
especially when you think of representing it as you feel it,
that is in such a way that it will make the same impression
on the public that it does on you, then you do not perceive the
lines on the wallpaper over there. Isn't that so? And when
you contemplate the whole thing you wouldn't dream of
counting the scales on the salmon, would you? You must see
them in the form of small silver pearls against grey and rose
colors! . . . As to the grapes! . . . What is striking is their tone
of light amber and the dust which models forms while soften-
ing them. It is the brightness of the tablecloth as well as the
spots which are not directly touched by the light which have
to be rendered . . . ." [27]

The most important Frenchwoman Impressionist, Berthe
Morisot, became Mary's friend. They were both well-to-do and
so were not compelled to spend valuable time trying to sell
their paintings, as was necessary for some of their colleagues.
Both were meticulous in their work. Berthe Morisot's repose,

as in the Manet portrait of her so entitled, was in contrast to Mary's energy and drive. Berthe was the great-granddaughter of the eighteenth-century painter Fragonard, of whom the de Goncourts wrote: He was "the audacious raconteur, the gallant *amoroso*, pagan and playful, whose wit was Gallic, whose genius was almost Italian, whose bright intelligence was French . . . ." [28] Some of these qualities Berthe had inherited. One commentator called her "the most fascinating figure of Impressionism." [29] She exhibited at the Salon from 1865 until 1874, when she became an Impressionist for the rest of her life. This was again in contrast to Mary Cassatt, who went on from Impressionism to other things and so in the long run could no more be called an Impressionist than could Degas.

Of the years just preceding Mary's arrival in Paris, Rewald wrote of Berthe Morisot: "Beyond the stage of early promises, her talent now emerged as that of a major artist in full possession of her means, gifted with an extraordinary sensitivity that lacked neither assurance nor temerity." [30] Devoted to Manet, Berthe married his brother Eugène. In her published correspondence there are several references to Mary. On one occasion Berthe's husband met the young American at an exhibition. "Mlle Cassatt . . . seemed to me to wish to keep in closer touch," he wrote his wife. "She asked if she might paint the baby's picture and yours. I told her gladly on condition of reciprocity." [31] At another time Berthe wrote her brother: "If you will talk to Mlle Cassatt she will perhaps be useful to you, 13, avenue Trudaine; she is intelligent." [32] Again she sent good wishes to Mary through Mallarmé, who told her that Mary appeared to count on her greatly. Another time Mallarmé reported that he had seen Mlle Cassatt at a concert wearing the flowers Berthe had sent her.

Less well in this early period Mary knew Renoir and Monet.

Cézanne as a person was comparatively a stranger to her. The Durand-Ruels were her good friends as well as her dealers. In fact the Durand-Ruels were a bulwark not only to herself but to a number of her colleagues who were striving for recognition in this difficult period. After the Franco-Prussian War, Paul Durand-Ruel not only continued his father's practice of buying the masters of the Barbizon School — Corot, Daubigny, Courbet and others — but he became increasingly interested in the new men and was to become as stubbornly enthusiastic and as persistent in their behalf as his father had been for artists of the older generation. Increasingly he identified his interest with theirs, though it was some time before he succeeded in selling their work. It was Durand-Ruel's belief, however, that "a true picture dealer should also be an enlightened patron; that he should, if necessary, sacrifice his immediate interest to his artistic convictions, and prefer to oppose, rather than support the interests of the speculators." [33]

Finally, in this period of Mary's life, there were her family, resident in Paris. They were her home, her dearly loved companions. They also came to be, especially when ill, her heavy responsibility.

Chapter II

IMPRESSIONISM AND INDEPENDENT ARTISTS

It was Degas who took the initiative in asking Mary Cassatt to show her work in the fourth Impressionist exhibition and it was he who made a list of her pictures to be shown. This service by a man noted for his negative attitude toward most activities that did not concern himself suggests how intrigued he was by the young American woman who felt as he did. He and she were becoming great friends. The show was held at 28 rue de l'Opera from April 10 to May 11, 1879. There were sixteen participants including, among others, Bracquemond, Caillebotte, Degas, Monet, Pissarro and Rouart. Gauguin showed, but arrived too late to be included in the catalogue. Berthe Morisot did not exhibit because she was expecting a child. The catalogue as finally printed gave Mary Cassatt's name without the picture titles.

This was her first showing with her new friends. She contributed *La Loge,* a young girl luminous in light and color, a mirror behind her head reflecting the interior of the theatre. After the show Alexis Rouart, a friend of Degas, purchased the painting. She also exhibited a picture of her sister Lydia seated in an armchair with a flowerbox in the background

Private Collection, Paris
Photograph from Durand-Ruel, Paris

La Loge

At the Opera

(now in the Metropolitan Museum, New York). Both pictures differ from her first two Salon paintings. There is a new ease, a soft blurring of some of the outlines, though the essential lines are there, and a feeling for firm structure. Women and girls at the theatre were favorite subjects for artists at this time. Mary painted also *At the Opera* (The Boston Museum of Fine Arts), a young woman in black leaning on the rail of her box, surveying the scene through opera glasses.

As a whole the exhibition had as hostile a reception and as bad reviews as its predecessors. Duranty's article made favorable mention of Mary Cassatt. Huysmans also spoke of her; writing about the show as a whole, he did not deny there might be some exhibitors who were not sufficiently skilled "... but take a man of great talent like M. Degas, take even his pupil, Mlle Mary Cassatt, and see if the works of these artists are not more interesting, more inquiring, more distinguished than all those trembling *machinettes* who hang ... in the interminable rooms of the Exposition. It is with these I find a real concern about contemporary life ...." [1]

Huysmans also explained "the generic terms" that he was forced to employ though he was aware that there was injustice in arbitrarily cataloguing artists of talent. Still for the purposes of his articles he felt he had no alternative but to divide these painters into two camps: those called Impressionists, such as Pissarro, Monet, Sisley, Berthe Morisot, and those called *Indépendants* such as Degas, Mary Cassatt, Raffaëlli, Caillebotte. Huysmans believed such classifications were not always pertinent and raised difficult questions about such painters as Manet and Renoir. [2]

Admission fees to the fourth exhibition totalled a modest sum in excess of expenditures. Degas wrote Bracquemond after the show closed reporting 439.50 francs for each exhibitor, "which is quite good." With her share Mary bought a Degas and a Monet, both of which had been included in the show. About this time she sent two of her own pictures to the Society of American Artists in New York — perhaps the first Impressionist canvases to be shown in the United States. Her work was also exhibited at the Pennsylvania Academy of the Fine Arts in Philadelphia, as it had been twice before. She was not forgetting her country or her home city.

When the fourth Impressionist exhibition was over Degas returned to his plan for a journal to be called *Le Jour et La Nuit*. To Bracquemond he wrote the middle of May: "I spoke to Caillebotte about the journal. He is willing to guarantee for us. Come and talk it over with me. No time to lose." [3] And again: "We must discuss the journal. Pissarro and I together made various attempts of which one [print] by Pissarro is a success. At the moment Mlle Cassatt is full of it. Impossible for me with my living to earn, to devote myself entirely to it as yet." [4] To the disappointment of his colleagues, the journal was to be a stillborn project.

Mary was occupied with other things as well. About this time she painted her self-portrait. It is a gouache and shows the influence of Degas. In a larger canvas, *Woman and Child Driving* (The Philadelphia Museum of Art), her sister and a little niece of Degas' are driving in a pony cart with the groom up behind. That other work was in progress is evident from a letter of Degas' to Bracquemond: "Tell Haviland who was infatuated with a little picture of Mlle Cassat [sic] and who wished to know the price, that it is a simple matter of 300 frcs, that he should write to me if that does not suit him and to Mlle Cassat, 6, Boulevard de Clichy if it does." [5]

With the fourth exhibition of the Impressionists began Mary Cassatt's showing of her paintings in exhibits to which

Degas also sent his work. By his colleagues Degas was regarded as often a difficult person. His quick fury lashed at them, his caustic and cruel wit victimized them, he would exert himself at times to spread a paralyzing gloom. Mary was not immune. To a friend she wrote: "Degas is a pessimist, and dissolves one (*il dissout*) so that you feel after being with him — oh, why try, since nothing can be done; — and this effect Gustave Moreau so felt that after a long friendship he said — 'After all, I may be wrong but I see things a certain way, and I simply cannot see you [Degas], you upset and discourage me.' " [6]

With this statement should go another to make more understandable Mary Cassatt's long friendship with Degas. Perhaps the other side of his character — a side Mary knew well — was best described in Daniel Halévy's Introduction to an edition of Degas' letters to his close friends: "The Degas who is revealed here is the artist and the friend . . . . The indefatigable friend: to attend a funeral, to clasp a hand Degas took the train and travelled 15 hours and all beneath the cover of a mask of insensibility, beneath uncouth habits, which did not touch the depths. 'My hard heart melts all the same,' he wrote about a stricken friend. But the mask was immediately resumed. 'What is this I hear' he cried one day bursting like a whirlwind upon a young and charming woman, one of his favorite hostesses, and called out from the doorstep 'what is this! I hear you are saying everywhere that I am not bad, that people are mistaken in me! If you take that away what will be left to me?' — There will be left, there is left the man who wrote these letters." [7] To this may be added an excerpt from a letter (included in the volume) that Degas wrote to his older friend, De Valernes: "Here I must ask your pardon for a thing which often comes up in your conversation and more often still in your thoughts: it is to have been during our long relationship to art, or to have seemed to be *hard* with you.

"I have been unusually so with myself, you must be fully aware of this seeing that you were constrained to reproach me with it and to be surprised that I had so little confidence in myself.

"I was or I seemed to be hard with everyone through a sort of passion for brutality, which came from my uncertainty and my bad humor. I felt myself so badly made, so badly equipped, so weak, whereas it seemed to me, that my calculations on art were so right. I brooded against the whole world and against myself. I ask your parden sincerely if, beneath the pretext of this damned art, I have wounded your very intelligent and fine mind, perhaps even your heart." [8]

As to the personal side of the friendship between Mary and Degas not much is known. "They went out together, dined together, and Degas examined at great length Mary's works in her atelier; he went with her to the Louvre and in the exhibitions." [9] Pierre Cabanne in his biography of Degas says: "Faithful to his principle: 'A painter has no private life,' Degas never married. To our knowledge he never had a love affair." [10] Cabanne then repeats the well-known story that when someone asked Degas why he had not married, he replied: "I'd be too afraid of hearing my wife say in front of one of my paintings, 'Very pretty what you're doing there.' " [11]

There had been a time when, in theory at least, he had not ruled out marriage. At the age of twenty he had recorded in his *Carnet:* "Could I find a nice little wife, someone simple and quiet [who] would understand my crazy ideas and with whom I could live while working at what I love best? There's a beautiful dream, isn't it?" More than a dozen years later the pos-

51703

sibility of marriage was still in his mind. By this time he had
recovered from the ill effects of his service during the Siege
of Paris — except for damage to his eyes — and had gone on
holiday to his brothers in New Orleans. From there he wrote
to Henri Rouart: "I long for order. I would not even consider
a good marriage inconsistent with my new approach to life.
To have children, my own children, would that be too much?
No. I dream of something well done, a well-ordered whole (in
the style of Poussin), and the old age of Corot. Now is the
time, this very moment. If not, life will continue in an orderly
way, but not so gay, not so respectable and full of regrets." [12]
Later he was to say, "There is love and there is creative work;
but a man has only one heart." [13]

Cabanne asks, "What sort of emotional life did Degas
have?" And answers, "Except for his affair with Mary Cassatt
of which we know very little, there were no women in Degas'
life. There are no letters and moreover no confession was ever
made which could shed some light on this aspect of his existence. Women are in his work, not in his life, and even then,
their presence often seems an instrument for discovering the
'real,' an object, often deprived of grace, sometimes formless,
which he used for his unending analyses . . . ." [14] Later in the
book he says of Degas and Mary Cassatt, "The similarity of
their taste, '*identical intellectual dispositions and identical
predilection for drawing*,' were to transform their friendly relations into a love affair, the duration and intensity of which
we know nothing." [15]

On Mary Cassatt's side, the picture is no clearer. After her
death it was found that she had destroyed his letters to her.
There were members of her family who believed Degas wanted
to marry her. At any rate, their friendship was to last for nearly
forty years. Sometimes they would see each other daily, some-

times not for months, and once when he said something about her work that offended her, she stopped seeing him for a much longer time. Their relationship was of interest to their friends, who now and again exerted themselves to bring the two back to friendly terms when a sharp disagreement had estranged them. In the opinion of one commentator: "So the state of their friendship was like a changing magnetic field in which objects are given motion by attraction and repulsion. There were no tragedies or scandals. Their love simply grew into a part of the artistic life of Paris." [16]

Mrs. Havemeyer once asked Mary how she managed to get along with Degas. She said her friend replied, "Oh, I am independent! I can live alone and I love to work. Sometimes it made him furious that he could not find a chink in my armor, and there would be months when we just could not see each other, and then something I painted would bring us together again and he would go to Durand-Ruel's and say something nice about me, or come to see me himself. When he saw my *Boy Before the Mirror* he said to Durand-Ruel: 'Where is she? I must see her at once. It is the greatest picture of the century.' When I saw him he went over all the details of the picture with me and expressed great admiration for it, and then, as if regretting what he had said, he relentlessly added: 'It has all your qualities and all your faults — *c'est l'Enfant Jésus et sa bonne anglaise.'* "

Mrs. Havemeyer asked, "Did no one ever hit him back?"

"Oh! certainly but Degas never cared. When criticism was at its worst, he said to me, '*Ils sont tous jaloux de nous. Ils veulent nous voler notre art.*' (They are jealous of us, and wish to steal our art.)"

" 'But,' continued Miss Cassatt after a quiet moment, and I [Mrs. Havemeyer] saw her face light up with a beautiful expression, 'magnificent! And however dreadful he was, he always lived up to his ideals.' Miss Cassatt folded her hands and I saw she had said all she cared to for the moment." [17]

As for Degas' influence on her work, Mellario expressed what seems to have been the general view: "Mary Cassatt came, one may say naturally, toward the impressionist group because her viewpoint already predisposed her to a clearing up of the pallette; because, after all, she was impatient with useless fetters and enthusiastic about the freedom of art. But when she wished to school herself seriously, to give to her individuality a more established and more pronounced character, the Master whose works interested her profoundly, whose advice she asked — a habit to which she was little accustomed — with whom she was largely in accord, was Degas.

"With a different temperament, not having to be concerned about maintaining her own originality, so long as she was spontaneous and alert, Mary Cassatt could profit from the intimacy, always formidable, with an artist of great talent, possessing both a biting character and very strong willpower. Certainly, neither by choice of subjects nor by the general aspect of painting, no more than in feeling and expression, did she show herself a docile follower. But, conscientious disciple, she learned from Degas concern for form and for movement, a horror of approximation and of meaningless detail . . . ." [18]

Neither Berthe Morisot nor Mary Cassatt wished her name to appear on the posters announcing the fifth group exhibition (1880). In their era, women were not accustomed to public display of their identities on billboards. Degas had lost his battle with Caillebotte about publishing any names at all, and several appeared. Degas was in despair. "When on earth will they stop the headlines? . . . All the good reasons and the good taste in the world can achieve nothing against the inertia of the others and the obstinacy of Caillebotte. . . . I am miserable about it, humiliated." [19]

At the sixth exhibition Mary met with some success. The difficult, hostile, caustic critic of *Le Figaro*, Albert Wolff, singled her out for special and more lenient mention. After stating that when he entered the exhibition it seemed to him he was penetrating an asylum for sick spirits, he went on to say that some were a trifle nearer sound thinking than others — lucid, brilliant — but that always their work was spoiled by some derangement. "From this scientific viewpoint, Miss Cassatt is a true phenomenon; in more than one of her canvases she is on the verge of becoming a notable artist with unparalleled natural feeling, penetrating observation and a welcome subjection before the model which is the accomplishment of peerless artists; then when that fine intelligence has served her well and is in repose, the little derangement takes over her palette and brushes and leaves his imprint on the work by improbable touches or by some flaws of color which have no reason for being — always by a deformed or monstrous spot which is blood-curdling and which makes one cry, What misfortune!

"What I have just said about Mlle Cassatt, who gives some flair to the group of Independents, applies equally to Mlle Morisot and, above all, to M. Degas . . . ." [20]

Gradually disagreement and division increased among the group. Pissarro wrote his son Lucien that Impressionism "really should be nothing more than a theory of observation, without entailing the loss of fantasy, freedom, grandeur, all that makes for great art. But not *eccentricity* to make sensitive people swoon." [21] The question as to who was eccentric and who was not was part of the problem, and theoretical differences were acerbated by personal animosities. Mary took no part in these dissensions, but when Degas refused to exhibit in the seventh show (1882) she followed his example. She was in touch with what was going on and was aware of the cross-pullings and acrimonious disputes, but it was her own work that absorbed her. She was working from eight in the morning until darkness put a stop to painting. In the evenings by artificial light she turned to etching in order to train herself in precision of line.

Following the crash of 1882, however, Mary Cassatt took a substantial but still inconspicuous part in aiding her fellow artists and in promoting Impressionism. The relative prosperity that had gained a foothold in France after the Franco-Prussian War had been a blessing to members of the group. Durand-Ruel had begun to buy paintings on a regular basis and arranged the financing so that a painter received a regular payment each month. After the crash, he was forced to abandon this practice and even to refuse to take all the paintings his artists produced. This resulted in severe hardships for several individuals. Mary helped in any way she could, buying pictures herself, urging her American friends to buy them, seeking to promote exhibitions in New York. At one point when Durand-Ruel found himself so overstocked with unsalable paintings and so deeply in debt that he faced bankruptcy, she came to his rescue with a loan.

Nor did she cease to be alert to the needs of America for fine pictures. When Mrs. Havemeyer was in Paris, she undertook to interest her in Courbet. Taking her to an exhibition of his work in the foyer of the Théâtre de la Gaîté, she talked about the excellence of his execution, his use of color and his realism. She led her friend to a beautiful nude, a woman pulling down a cherry branch across her face. "Did you ever see such flesh painting?" Mary Cassatt asked. "Look at her bosom

— it lives, it is almost *too* real!" And she added, "The Parisians don't care for him. You must have one of his nude half-lengths some day!" [22] Subsequently Mrs. Havemeyer bought this Courbet, as well as others.

Mary kept her brother Aleck in mind also as a picture buyer. Evidently there had been some correspondence about the possible purchase of one particular Degas, for her mother wrote him: "I don't know whether Mary has written to you or not on the subject of pictures. I don't encourage her much as to buying the large one, being afraid that it would be too big for anything but a gallery or a room with a great many pictures in it — but as it is unfinished or, rather, as a part of it has been washed out and Degas imagines he cannot retouch it without painting the whole over again — and he cannot make up his mind to do that — I doubt if he ever sells it. He says it is one of those works which are sold after a man's death and artists buy them not caring whether they are finished or not. It is the same with a picture of danseuses which Mary would like to buy for you — he says he must repaint it all merely because a small portion has been washed out .... Mary is keeping a look-out and whenever she sees anything of his or anyone else's which she thinks you would like at what she thinks reasonable prices she will buy them. She says she is afraid to order anything from Degas as he might make something so eccentric you might not like it."

To her brother Mary wrote privately: "Did you get the photographs I sent you? I only sent them to give you an idea of Degas' style. I don't like to buy anything for you without your having some idea of what it would be like. The pictures from which the photographs were taken have all been sold and Degas has but one racing picture finished and that is the large one; I was just thinking of buying you a smaller picture of

A Cup of Tea

ladies and children on horseback when a dealer picked it up and I don't see anything else in horse subjects that I can get for you just at present. I feel it almost too much of a responsibility, am afraid you won't like my selection, and Mother does not give me much encouragement as 'au fond' I think she believes picture buying to be great extravagance."

Mary was now frequently using members of her family as models. Among the paintings that she exhibited at this time was A *Cup of Tea* (The Boston Museum of Fine Arts), a picture of Lydia and a guest. They are seated on a sofa behind a silver tea service.* This silver had been a wedding present belonging to Mary's grandmother, Mary Stevenson, for whom she was named. The Boston Museum wrote at the time it purchased this picture that it was "full of air, light and pure color; the figures are treated with directness and lack of sentimentality; the drawing and composition are sound and forceful . . . . A *Cup of Tea* does not depend on strange or new subjectmatter to obtain its unique quality, but gains it entirely from sincerity of approach and mastery of technique." [23]

The same year she painted *Woman Reading in a Garden* (The Art Institute of Chicago). At the time of purchase it was said: "The painting, celebrating a theme dear to the painters of this group and to Monet and Manet in particular, shows the artist at the height of her Impressionist phase. The background of richly blooming roses gives a brilliant color note against which the delicate whites and greys of the figure in its light dress contrast with distinction. The intensity of the color and the flooding light are suggestive of Renoir, a Master who influenced Mary Cassatt considerably at this time . . . ." [24]

It was probably during the year when neither she nor Degas

---

* *Of this Lemoisne remarked, "In an amusing arrangement on the canvas, the tea tray occupies the first plane." Degas et Son Oeuvre, Vol. I, p. 191.*

Courtesy Mrs. Eric de Spoelberch
Haverford, Pennsylvania

Reading *Le Figaro* (Mary Cassatt's Mother)

exhibited with the group that she painted a picture of her mother, *Reading Le Figaro*. According to Sweet, this oil "marks the culmination of Mary Cassatt's earlier period. The picture is painted with broad, fluid brushstrokes, the figure is solidly, in fact, monumentally conceived and the deep concentration of the sitter gives a feeling of great psychological intensity." [25]

During the crash of 1882 Mary did not have the financial troubles that afflicted most of her painter friends. She did not have to borrow money from acquaintances or patrons as did Monet; she did not have to spend precious time walking the streets of Paris from one dealer to another trying to sell canvases as did Pissarro. Nonetheless her work was seriously interrupted. Her sister Lydia, increasingly unwell, became gravely ill, and it was she who nursed her. When the worst was temporarily over, Mary sat down and wrote to Aleck: "It was on Tuesday that the worst attack came. She lay with her eyes wide open and totally blind, and remained so for twenty-four hours. Of course it seemed to us the end . . . . However, this time it was not so." Mary and her father had been told by the doctor that Lydia could not get well. "Mother has not been told anything about it yet. I keep her spirits up as well as I can and thus far she bears it better than I thought she would, is really not much alarmed. But she is very much fatigued. However, I don't allow her to sit up at night at all and make her lie down as much in the daytime as possible. We are trying to get a nurse. The doctor insists upon it so evidently they think the illness will be a long one and they say I won't be able to stand it alone and Mother must not be allowed to do anything. . . . Give my love to all and excuse this letter but I am so tired I can hardly hold a pen."

By mid-September Lydia developed new and alarming symptoms, though the nature of her malady is unknown. She as well as the rest of the family began to recognize her danger. Her father wrote to Aleck that Lydia had "lately spoken to Mary of her probable death and made her promise to have her buried in the country and directed her to give keepsakes to you and Gard. Poor dear!" Though they now had a trained nurse, Mary was also carrying part of the care. Her father wrote, "Lydia says she has developed into a most excellent nurse. — As far as her art is concerned the summer has been lost to her."

Lydia died in November. Mary was so stricken she could not for some time resume her work. Responding to the cabled news, Aleck with his wife and children left for France the day after Lydia's death. When they arrived in Paris some two weeks later, Mary found comfort in her brother's presence and in the children's company. Though she and Aleck's wife seldom saw eye to eye, Lois wrote her mother from Paris: "Mary seems to be most anxious to be friendly and proposes something for us to do together every day. She is very lonesome . . . and says she feels now that perhaps she would have been better off to have married when she thinks of being left alone in the world. She has not had the heart to touch her painting for six months and she will scarcely now be persuaded to begin. She will however begin a picture of Aleck soon, I think . . . ."

When spring came, it was Mary's hope that she and her mother might go to London the last week in May to see Durand-Ruel's exhibition. At Dowdeswell's galleries in New Bond Street he was showing works by Pissarro, Renoir, Sisley, Monet, Degas, Berthe Morisot, Manet and two of her own. Lucien Pissarro, writing his father from London, said that the majority of the papers did not like the Impressionists. Still "people talk about it, come to see and laugh — that's already something. There were always crowds every time I went." [26] Though most of the critics did not like the show, an article in *The Standard*, London, for April 25 stated in part: "When fault-finding is over there remains great reason to welcome the exhibition as a whole. It sets before us much better than has hitherto been set before us the aims and achievements of a modern school of undoubted importance. The Impressionists are not all that narrow, ill-informed, and partisan advocacy has represented them to be . . . . With all their deficiencies, they are individual, brilliant, engaging. They are a force to be reckoned with. And one of the greatest causes of their force is that it is the life of their own day that has inspired their art." [27]

The spring of 1883 was saddened for Mary by Manet's death. Staunch admirer of his best work, she was instrumental in securing some of his finest pictures for America. She also felt his connection with the happy change in her own work when she decided against the Salon and associated herself with the independent movement even though Manet himself held back from such identification. Even Degas, who had frequently crossed swords with Manet, mournfully admitted, "He was greater than we thought." [28]

In 1883 Mary painted *Young Woman in Black*, of which a critic wrote that it was "singularly notable, not only for the solidity of both the woman's figure and the composition but for the delicacy of such tonal passages as the right side of her face; the enormously sensitive brushing of her black gown; the manner in which it is framed by the vividly patterned chair, and the way in which, bold as it is, that mass of black is still kept, by the bold geometrical patterning of the background and the delicate design of the chair, from dominating the composition." [29]

In mid-June Mary Cassatt had an operation. That it was not too serious may be judged from a report to his mother by her young nephew, Eddie, who was staying at her house: "Aunt Mary had an operation performed at Deauville. She is going to buy another horse. They are going to sell Bichette .... Grandfather has gone to England .... Tell Sis we have good strawberries and asparagus yet."

Eddie was also responsible for an account of Whistler's visit to the Cassatts. He had been working on a portrait of Aleck's wife, and early in May he came to call. Wrote Eddie: "We had a visit from Whistler last night. I was not here but they told me about him. He came with a cane about three feet and a half high and a glass in his eye. When they told him that little Mary Scott was being painted by Millais, he said, 'Poor little thing. I pity her.' Talking about Mama's portrait he said, 'I think on the whole when I come to think it over, I like it better than anything I have done.' Grandmother told him that she thought no woman looks as well in a riding habit as out of it. Says he, 'Oh it depends on the artist that paints her.' He was at Mr. Degas' yesterday and Degas asked him how old he was. Oscar Wilde and another satellite that was there burst out laughing. Whistler answered, 'Twenty-two' .... Oh he is an idiot. Oscar Wilde and he together are just as crazy a pair of men as can be found on the face of the earth ...."

The saga of Whistler's portrait of Lois Cassatt was to continue far beyond this spring of 1883. In the fall, Mary was in London, and when she returned home wrote to her brother about her visit to Whistler's studio. Whistler himself had been out of town, but he had insisted that one of his pupils

Courtesy Art Association of Indianapolis
Herron Museum of Art

Young Girls

be sent for "to show me the studio. The portrait is not quite done yet. I thought it a fine picture, the figure especially, beautifully drawn. I don't think it by any means a striking likeness, the head inferior to the rest. The face has no animation but that I believe he does on purpose. He does not talk to his sitters, but sacrifices the head to the ensemble. He told Mother — she, you know, went up to London before me and saw him at his studio — he told her that he would have liked a few more sittings, that he felt as if he was working against time; that, I suppose, is true enough. I told his pupil that you were very anxious to have the picture and that I hoped he would soon send it to you. After all I don't think you could have done better. It is a work of Art and as young Sargent said to Mother this afternoon, it is a good thing to have a portrait by Whistler in the family."

The end of the following year, when Aleck was in Paris, Mary wrote Lois that he was going on to England shortly to stay for a week. "I hope Aleck will get Whistler to give up your portrait. He is now working on it I hear . . . . I am sorry you don't like it. You remember I recommended Renoir but neither you nor Aleck liked what you saw of his. I think Whistler's picture very fine."

No doubt it was Mary herself who regaled her nephew Eddie with the details of Whistler's visit. She had a way with children. She loved them as naturally and as unsentimentally as she loved horses and dogs. But she expected more of them — expected and usually got it. While Eddie was living with them, it was simply assumed he would do his homework every evening. He did do it without fuss or prompting and then was much pleased with his good academic standing. But Mary's interests were never entirely in books for young students, and soon she was writing Aleck that she hoped Eddie's mother would "reconsider her orders not to let him play cricket on Sunday afternoon — tell her I am afraid he will be very dull with only us to talk to."

When the young came to visit her, she put her mind on making life pleasant for them. From Marly one summer morning she took four nephews and nieces to Versailles "all in a great gig." When Aleck planned to leave his brood at the Cassatts' Paris home while he and his wife toured Italy, their mother exclaimed, "You never saw such preparations as they have made for them." At Beaufresne Mary provided her younger guests with a boat for the pond and with a pony for land work. True, it was the chauffeur who went with them in the boat, since their Aunt Mary was seasick even on a quiet body of water. When it came to gifts, mechanical toys intrigued her, and she carefully selected those she gave them for Christmas. As they grew older, a leather bag seemed the thing to give a great-niece commuting from home to school, and later a blue enamelled watch that could be worn also as a locket.

When she painted children, they were not idealized in the least. If they were a little ugly, they appear in the painting as a little ugly. As with her older models, she adapted them to the structure and pattern of her work. But the children kept their identity and there were never two alike.

Those were the days of nursemaids and governesses, so she did not have the care of children on a day-in-day-out basis. But had that been necessary she would probably have managed well. She was a skilled and devoted nurse when adults in her family were ill, and no child under her care would have lacked anything that was good for him. When little Tony and Alexander were expected at Beaufresne with their nurses, Mary wrote their mother: ". . . I will have a pineapple in the house. The juice is a cure for croup." Far from pampering, her attitude was one of bracing expectation. Whatever might go wrong, those involved would of course cooperate in making the best of it. When one of her visiting nephews picked up some adult pills from the breakfast table and dropped them into his brother's chocolate, Aunt Mary was no doubt "perfectly crazy" as the dropper gleefully wrote home. But the offense was not repeated.

Meanwhile Mary was trying to sell her paintings in America. While she worked in her studio, she persuaded her mother to write Aleck asking him to straighten out matters with an art dealer in Philadelphia who had a number of her canvases. "Mary has written to him over and over again and he has never troubled himself to reply but once and then it was months after she had written." Apparently the dealer "has an idea that it is of no consequence to Mary whether she sells or not and so holds on for higher prices in spite of all she says to him . . . . I can't bear to trouble you but we want to be done with this thing once and for all. Mary wants all her smaller pictures sold at auction either in New York or Philadelphia, two or three at a time at every important sale that may take place until they are all sold. The three or four larger ones . . . she says are good enough to bring high prices and if [the dealer] can't or won't sell them she will make arrangements to send them to somebody else. After they are sold she will never send anything except to New York where there is some chance and where she is known and acknowledged to have some talent. In Philadelphia it is the case of 'a prophet is never without honor' etc."

Chapter III

THE LAST GROUP EXHIBITION; SHOWINGS IN NEW YORK

During the late winter and early spring of 1884, Mary Cassatt could not paint. Her time and attention were consumed by her mother's illness, by her efforts to find a new place for them to live and by problems of relocating her family. These four months of professional inactivity started off well, however, with no sign of difficulties ahead. Mrs. Cassatt's doctor prescribed a change of climate, and in December Mary and her mother went to Spain. Mary was open-minded about the trip. There was a possibility of course that it would prove beneficial. Personally she thought her mother's ill health was largely due to the five flights of stairs she had to climb to reach their Paris apartment. "Father does not feel them," she wrote Aleck from Tarragon, "and thinks nobody else ought to." She urged her brother to write him that this climb was too difficult for their mother and to express the hope that they would soon move into a house with a lift.

But more than stairs proved to be the matter with her mother, who took to her bed as soon as they arrived in Spain. Even as Mary wrote home, they were waiting for the doctor. "We have got to the right place for climate," she told Aleck.

"It is perfectly delicious here like the most delicious spring weather. The town is on a rock some eight hundred feet high, on the Mediterranean about four hours from Barcelona. It is one of the oldest places in Spain, built by the Carthaginians, the walls still standing. It is picturesque beyond description and the country around most beautiful, not in the least like Italy — much grander; if it were not for Mother's health it would be most enjoyable." Before leaving Paris, she had found a beautiful Manet for Aleck. "Manet's sale takes place next month and I told Portier what to buy for you if the prices were low enough . . . . You cannot do better and as long as you have begun to get a few pictures you might as well go on. My poor painting is sadly interrupted. I have no time now for anything and the constant anxiety takes all heart out of me; my only hope is that this change will set Mother right for a time."

Presently her mother's cough entirely disappeared, and they moved on to Alicante where the Marquis Casa-Loring, a cousin of friends, was helpful. Though Mrs. Cassatt seemed to improve, she was determined to return home, and the marquis sent to Madrid for a carriage for them. They had a compartment reserved for their journey, but Mrs. Cassatt could get no nearer home than Biarritz.

After three weeks there, she showed improvement and Mary was freer to enjoy whatever was available. "This place is full of English," she wrote early in March, "about a hundred in this hotel, some of the 'bluest blood' in England . . . . Alongside me at table I have an English clergyman who is a rich man as well; he is intelligent and tolerably well informed, but he cannot understand how they can give a dinner party in America where there is no 'precedence.' I propound difficult problems of precedence to him — he little imagines the inward amusement he affords me." She added, "You never saw anything like the economy of these English. Some of them actually live here for 10 francs a day, and this is a first-class hotel. I don't know how they manage it but they are awful screws. I am bored to death here as you may imagine, in fact I have had an awful winter but if Mother only gets well, I shan't mind anything...."

Mary stayed with her mother until the doctor assured her she would be safe in Mathilde's care. Then she returned to Paris to find new living quarters for the family. Arrangements for moving were complicated by the need to find someone to take over their unexpired lease at 13 avenue Trudaine and by the difficulties her father created. "He is harder to manage than he ever was in his life," she wrote Aleck. "It is most provoking that Father, the moment our backs are turned, had the notice taken down and refused to allow the place to be seen; for two people wanted it and would even have bought some of our fixtures, so the concierge says." Once moved, Mary was pleased with their new home, though it took some time for her father to make the adjustment. "Father went on like a crazy man for the first three weeks and nearly killed me .... He allowed me to do as I liked about furnishings — that is, about curtains and hangings and I began to be quite interested, but had to leave to come to Mother before anything was done and I don't know how things look. The house is very handsome and the rooms are nicely furnished and ceilings much higher than in avenue Trudaine." In the course of the negotiations she had been able to secure a third servant's room.

Back in Biarritz she found her mother miserable "and quite overcome at the sight of me. She felt herself rather abandoned, I am afraid." Two weeks later, her mother was able to leave her bed and lie on a sofa. Mr. Cassatt was impatient to have

them back again, and Mary hoped they might soon be able
to start for Paris. "You cannot imagine," she wrote Aleck,
"what it is to have beef tea made and try to tempt the appe-
tite in a hotel. Mathilde is a most devoted creature but she is
not so intelligent as she is devoted, nor has she much training
in nursing." As for herself, Mary reported, "I have been utterly
upset, have had violent toothache and a swollen face. Yesterday the dentist lanced the gum, but it seems worse today. I
think it is not only the tooth but all the worry and fatigue I
have had." She added: "When I was in Paris I found Portier
had sold two of my pictures and more were wanted but I have
not touched a brush since we left home and have not been out
of Mother's room except for a walk, since I have been here.
It will do me good to get to work again."

Two weeks later they were back in Paris. "We arrived home
safely this morning after a dreadful journey from Biarritz. The
heat was like summer heat at home and, under the impression
that Mother had inflammation of the lungs, I had her covered
with wadding. It is a wonder she did not die of the exertions
of breathing only . . . . If you could only imagine the relief it
is to get her home where we can get what we wish in the way
of food and where we have people to wait on us, and our
minds relieved."

Before long she was back at work, her studio the salon of
their new apartment. Among other things she did a portrait
of a family friend, "but I don't think it very good." She was
also working on the portrait of Aleck and his son Robert.*

Presently she was writing her older brother: "This morning
I went to see Degas and he insisted on my going to see the
exhibition at Petit's Gallery at once, as he wanted me to judge

* *This painting was auctioned in New York on April 15, 1959, and purchased for the Philadelphia Museum of Art for $39,000.*

Mary Cassatt at the Louvre, by Degas

of the effects of the Monets. They have managed to nearly kill him — they were up until three in the morning the day before the opening and every time one of Monet's pictures was hung the painters next took theirs away. Finally they separated all his pictures and put them in different corners!"

The end of June they were settled in the country at Arques-la-Bataille. "I think we are a little too near the sea for Mother but she insisted upon trying it and the house is low and sheltered. Aleck would be delighted with the country," Mary told his wife, "it is so like England — the beautiful part of England, hedges neatly trimmed, broad meadows, and everything very green. For my part I prefer the valley of the Oise."

Friends lived six or seven miles away and had expressed pleasure in the prospect of having the Cassatts for neighbors. To Aleck Mary wrote: "I rode over there to see them on Saturday. They have a pretty place — an English park . . . . The roads disappoint me very much. They are good carriage roads but nothing for riding and we have to be careful of our beautiful Isabella's legs. Last summer we had two forests near us where we could gallop for miles on soft ground." She continued: "Talking of horses we would like to be informed about the racing. Mother doesn't approve but still wishes to know all about it. The other day I had a good laugh at her. Gard * sent me two New York papers with an account of the exhibition. After reading about that Mother searched a good while and finally exclaimed with disappointment when she found we had only half the paper. She was hunting for the racing news!"

In the early fall, Mary gratified her father by doing a large pastel of him mounted on Isabella "with which he is much

* J. Gardner Cassatt, her younger brother.

delighted but he says you will never believe that she is as handsome as I have made her." Mary enjoyed riding Isabella as much as her father did and had her own saddle. She told her brother that a friend was ordering one exactly like it — ". . . he thinks it the best saddle he ever saw." When Eddie was making her home his headquarters while he attended the École Spéciale Militaire at St. Cyr, she rode with him in the Bois. On one occasion Eddie wrote his mother, "Aunt Mary was tickled to death because an officer of Engineers admired her mare and stopped to tell me so."

She rode wherever and whenever she could. Degas, receiving a reply from her to one of his letters, wrote a mutual friend: ". . . whilst riding in the forest and having got lost among the rocks, her mare shied and she thought she saw her steed's leg already swollen. It was a viper. It appears," Degas added, "that a viper is healthier for animals than it is for us and that it does not kill." [1]

Often she doctored her horses herself. She reported to Aleck that Isabella had gone lame, but assured him that she was treating her with success. "But if I trot too much then she limps a little the next day. It comes from a windgall on her right foreleg and the end of it will be that we will put her in the carriage and sell old Joe. She is younger and far better than he is. He is getting cranky. Last spring we were going to sell him and try another and Father went to —— to bid on a colt he thought would do. It seems he (the colt) was handsomer, eleven years old and he had windgalls too. But Father thought him worth 1200 francs and was prepared to pay that much for him. He sold for 5280 francs. I am glad someone else got him and his windgalls. Father cares nothing for windgalls — he says all horses had them when he was young. The fact is all he cares for is beauty. I read out to him from the *Turf and Field* the other day, the editor's remark that he preferred a plain trotter to a horse who was happiest when he was posed before a looking glass."

Though the Cassatts had their own coachman, Mary loved to drive herself, especially with the horses in tandem. When a carriage horse grew too old for use, the parting was sad, though none of the Cassatts were sentimental in their fondness for animals. Once when Gard was visiting her, an order had to be given the groom to have one of their horses destroyed. Later in the week when she was out walking with Gard they passed a hack stand. Suddenly Mary pointed to a horse hitched to a public conveyance, then hurried forward to pat their old pet. Instead of obeying orders, the groom had sold the horse for his own gain. Immediately Mary repurchased the horse and discharged the groom.

As for the races, Mary did not often have time to go, but she kept an eye on the entries and wished her young relatives a successful experience when they headed for the racetrack. One afternoon while Eddie was there she did go with him to the Grand-Prix. They came home "looking like millers, actually white with dust." Another day she wrote home: "Father and I went to the first day's races here . . . . The ground is lovely — a beautiful green meadow with hills on either side. There were not a great many people there the first day but it was a beautiful sight. I must say I think Degas has done some very fine pictures of races. It is a pity he has given it up . . . ."

Mary's own riding days came to an abrupt end. Degas wrote about it to his friend, Henri Rouart: ". . . Tillot must have written to you that poor Mlle Cassatt had a fall from her horse, broke the tibia of her right leg and dislocated her left shoulder . . . . She is going on well, and here she is for a long time to come, first of all immobilized for many long summer weeks and then deprived of her active life and perhaps also of her horsewoman's passion. The horse must have put its foot in a hole made by the rain on soft earth." [2]

Meanwhile Mary Cassatt had a social obligation on her mind. When she and her mother had been in London attending the Impressionist exhibition and viewing Whistler's portrait of Lois Cassatt, their cousin, Mrs. Riddle, and her daughter, Annie Scott, insisted on having them as guests. One day when they were all shopping, Mary saw a lovely old Japanese tea and coffee set which she admired. No sooner was she back in Paris than the set arrived — a gift. She was delighted but soon wondered how she could repay such kindness. When their cousins eventually came to Paris she suggested that Mrs. Riddle sit to her for a portrait. Both she and her daughter were pleased, and the sittings began. Presently Mrs. Cassatt wrote Aleck: "The picture is nearly done but Mary is waiting for a very handsome Louis XVI frame to be cut down to suit before showing it to them. As they are not very artistic in their likes and dislikes of pictures and as a likeness is a hard thing to make to please the nearest friends, I don't know what the results will be. Annie ought to like it in one respect for both Degas and Raffaëlli said it was 'La distinction même!' "

Mrs. Cassatt's doubts of the reception of the portrait were justified. The family were not pleased with the picture.* Mary was terribly disappointed. "I felt I never wanted to see it again." Years later, on the eve of the war, Mrs. Havemeyer suggested that Miss Cassatt go through her storage closets and see what came to light. When Mrs. Havemeyer saw this pic-

---

* Mary's brother Aleck wrote from Paris to his wife: "Mary has done an excellent portrait of Mrs. Riddle, quite as good in its way as the one we have of Mother, but I don't think Mrs. Scott quite likes it."

ture, *Lady at the Tea Table,* she demanded, "Why have you never shown it before?"

Mary explained about the family's disapproval. "I did it so carefully and you may be sure it was like her . . . ."

"Well, I care about it," Mrs. Havemeyer said hotly, "and so will others." She insisted it be shown and Mary finally yielded to her judgment. Triumphantly Mrs. Havemeyer recorded: "It was the sensation of the exhibit in the Rue Lafitte in 1914 with the result that both the Luxembourg and the Petit Palais were anxious to have it." [3] This was not the first time the Luxembourg had wanted one of her paintings. Some time before, she had written to a friend that Durand-Ruel had given a "decided refusal to sell one of my pictures in his private collection to the Luxembourg, which ends my hope of immortality in that direction!" [4] Even so, it must have pleased her that Durand-Ruel wanted to keep her work. However, Mary refused to let her *Lady at the Tea Table* go to either of these French galleries. She had other plans for it. Eventually she gave it to the Metropolitan Museum in New York.

The year that she painted *Lady at the Tea Table* (1883) was also notable for two marriages — that of her brother Gardner to Eugenia Carter,* and that of her friend Louisine Waldron Elder to Henry O. Havemeyer of the famous "Sugar Trust." Both the Havemeyers were to become discriminating and substantial patrons of the arts, with Mary Cassatt frequently their consultant and adviser.

In 1886 she showed at the eighth Impressionist exhibition. It was Berthe Morisot and her husband, Eugène Manet, who took the initiative in promoting this last of the group shows, after Pissarro had discussed the possibility with both Mary

---

* *The Gardner Cassatts were to have three children: Gardner; Ellen Mary Cassatt (Mrs. Horace Binney Hare), and Eugenia.*

Cassatt and Monet.[5] Internal disagreement arose almost at once. Pissarro wanted to include his friends, Seurat and Signac, but this was not pleasing to some of the others. Soon the nub of the dispute centered in the showing of Seurat's *La Grande Jatte*. Pissarro wrote his son about the trouble he was having: ". . . I had a violent run-in with M. Eugène Manet on the subject of Seurat and Signac . . . . You may be sure I rated Manet roundly — which will not please Renoir. But anyhow this is the point: I explained to M. Manet, who probably didn't understand anything I said, that Seurat has something new to contribute which these gentlemen, despite their talent, are unable to appreciate, that I am personally convinced of the progressive character of his art and certain that in time it will yield extraordinary results . . . . I do not accept the snobbish judgment of 'romantic impressionists' to whose interest it is to combat new tendencies. I accept the challenge, that's all. But before anything is done they want to stack the cards and ruin the exhibition. M. Manet was beside himself! I didn't calm down. They are all underhanded, but I don't give in. Degas is a hundred times more loyal. I told Degas that Seurat's painting was very interesting. 'I would have noted that myself, Pissarro, except that the painting is so big!' Very well, if Degas sees nothing in it so much the worse for him. This simply means there is something precious that escapes him. M. Manet would have liked to prevent Seurat from showing his figure painting. I protested against this, telling Manet that in such a case we would make no concessions, that we were willing, if space were lacking, to *limit our paintings* ourselves, but that we would fight anyone who tried to impose his choice on us. But things will arrange themselves somehow!" [6]

The way they arranged themselves was that Pissarro exhibited in a separate room with Seurat, Signac, and his own son, Lucien, who showed watercolors and woodcuts.[7] Among those not exhibiting in this final showing were Monet, Caillebotte, Renoir and Sisley. There was also disagreement as to the best date for the show. Degas wanted it to be at the same time as the official Salon showing. Pissarro and others thought such timing would reduce their sales. "Miss Cassatt and Degas say this is no objection," he wrote his son, "but it's easy to talk that way when you don't have to wonder where your next meal will come from!" [8] Since Pissarro, Gauguin, Guillaumin and their friends could not themselves raise the funds needed for an exhibition, it was imperative to have the support of artists who were better off, such as Degas, Mary Cassatt and Berthe Morisot. "Degas doesn't have to sell," Pissarro wrote his son. "He will always have Miss Cassatt and not a few exhibitors outside our group." [9] The show was held, however, from May 15 to June 15 as Degas wished.

Though getting his way, Degas was not exultant. Some time before, he had written a friend that as he approached fifty he felt like an old man. ". . . One closes, like a door, and not only upon friends. One cuts off everything around one and, when quite alone, extinguishes — in a word, kills oneself out of disgust. I was so full of projects; here I am blocked, powerless. And furthermore I've lost the thread. I always thought I had time; what I didn't do, what I was prevented from doing — in the midst of all my difficulties and in spite of the weakness of my eyes — I never gave up hope of starting one fine day. I hoarded all my plans in a cupboard of which I always carried the key with me, and I've lost that key. Lastly, I feel that the state of coma I am in I shan't be able to throw off. I shall keep myself occupied, as those who do nothing say, and that will be all." [10]

Among the pictures shown at this exhibition was Mary

Girl Arranging her Hair (Morning Toilet)

Cassatt's *Morning Toilet* (The National Gallery of Art, Washington). She had painted this to show Degas how wrong he had been in making a belittling gesture that had vexed her. Together they had been viewing the work of another artist, and Mary had expressed the opinion that the man could not draw. Degas had shrugged in a way that implied, What can a woman know about drawing? For once his friend made no comment, but went back to her studio and set to work. By this time she had had much practice in drawing and she engraved directly on copper, discarding the whole if she made the slightest mistake. She would now paint a picture where line was emphasized.

She secured an unattractive model with no prettiness or charm to distract the observer. She had her wear a plain nightdress, placed her against a washstand in an undistinguished chair, and showed her how to hold her rather sparse hair. She arranged this adenoidal subject in the pose she wanted and went to work. When the picture was finished, she showed it to Degas. Instantly he exclaimed, "What drawing! What style!" and took possession of the picture for his own collection. Mary did not remind him of his slighting comment-by-gesture. But she was pleased by the outcome of her resolve to prove him wrong.

Mary Cassatt's personal disappointment that her work was not appreciated by most members of her family, and by the American public generally, did not slow her effort to win a following for the Impressionists and the independent painters. She wanted to see a group of discriminating people in her own country who would understand what her colleagues were doing. Most of all she wanted to help develop in the United States a more widespread appreciation of art generally. She knew this would take time; still she would do what she could to make paintings available. Public galleries were of course the ideal place, but the museum movement was not then far advanced, and only limited funds were available. She saw that a useful intermediate step was encouraging private collections. As her brother Aleck had an acute ear to the ground for the development of transportation, so she kept attuned to interest in art on the part of wealthy individuals. She believed that several of the private collections, then in process of building, would eventually find their way into galleries open to the public. Her role, as she saw it, was to induce as many wealthy friends as possible to purchase art.

To her great satisfaction several of these friends bought because they loved fine paintings. She also helped direct the purchases of those who themselves knew nothing about pictures. She had observed that the motives of such people were varied. Some wanted the prestige of owning a canvas that was accepted as a masterpiece. Some wanted to be associated as owners with a movement that was causing a stir in the art world; they wanted to be in the vanguard of whatever was going on. Others purchased pictures for commercial reasons, expecting their monetary value to increase.

To forward her plan of securing paintings for the United States, Mary not only interested compatriots she met in Paris — she also did much to promote exhibitions in New York. She knew there were large obstacles in her path. The conservative critics and their followers who had invested in Gérôme, Bouguereau, Cabanel and Meissonier were determined that the newcomers, who flouted the standards of the Salon, should gain no foothold in America. In 1886 Durand-Ruel showed many Impressionist paintings in New York: fifty by Monet, forty-two by Pissarro, thirty-eight by Renoir, fourteen by Sisley and nine by Berthe Morisot. With them he exhibited work by other independent artists: twenty-three by Degas, twenty-seven by Manet and two by Mary herself. Renoir and others believed that Mary Cassatt was at least indirectly responsible for this exhibition. His son quotes Renoir as saying that the Impressionists perhaps owed to the Americans their not dying of hunger. "The American public is probably no more alert than the French, but it doesn't think it necessary to sneer at things it doesn't understand." [11]

In an introduction to the catalogue for this 1886 exhibition Theodore Duret had written in part: "The Impressionists are the descendants of the naturalist painters: their fathers are Corot, Courbet and Manet." Also: "The Impressionists had borrowed from their immediate predecessors of the French School their honest way of painting in the open air, offhand, with vigorous touches; to these were added the bold and novel methods of coloring learned of the Japanese, and thus furnished they began to develop their own individuality and to look at nature with their own eyes."

The New York exhibition was shown first at the American Art Galleries and later moved to the National Academy of Design, where a number of additional paintings were shown, including the two by Mary Cassatt. The New York Herald reviewing the earlier show commented: "It is a pity Miss Mary Cassatt could not have been also represented." The same review insisted that the Impressionists did not need four galleries "to give a good idea of their eccentric methods of expressing, or often very nearly suppressing, the undoubted talents they all possess. The work of these artistic 'cranks' is much of it extremely interesting, and nearly all of it absurdly mannered . . . ." [12] From much of the condemnation Manet and Degas were excepted.

The *New York Daily Tribune* noted the opposition of the more conservative-minded who thought "the paintings of the Impressionists partake of the character of a 'crazy quilt,' being only distinguished by such eccentricities as blue grass, violently green skies and water with the coloring of a rainbow. In short it has been said that the paintings of this school are utterly and absolutely worthless. We do not find them so. On the contrary, we are disposed to blame the gentlemen who purvey pictures for the New York market for leaving the public in ignorance of the artists represented at the exhibition in the American Art Galleries. There is evidently more vitality and beauty in some of the paintings by Claude Monet, Pissarro, Renoir and Ferret, than in studio scrappings which Rousseau, Corot and their brothers, if alive, would be reluctant to father. There are technical lessons to be learned from the pictures of Manet and Degas which are worth something to every artist who has the power of intelligent discrimination. These pictures represent an interesting movement in foreign art, and the time has gone by for Americans to wait to learn of art movements from ancient history . . . When Delacroix and Gericault were leading the 'romantic' movement, and when Constable was influencing French art, Americans, placidly indifferent, collected 'old masters'. . . ." [13]

The New York Times, speaking of *A Portrait* by Mary Cassatt, said there was expression in the subject's face, "if the work as a whole is not particularly striking." And in summarizing "commendable achievements" it included her *Family Group*.[14] The *New York World*, after much unfavorable comment on the show generally, referred to the works added at the second exhibition: ". . . and Mary Cassatt's, a Philadelphia pupil of Degas,' *Family Group*, well composed and admirable in expression, and *Portrait of a Lady*, a well-conceived and executed study of whites and grays." The reviewer added, "These Impressionist works cannot be given too much study by any person who is at all interested in art." [15] The *New York Herald* referred to "two works by Mary Cassatt, one of the few American members of the impressionistic group. Like Madame Morisot she is a woman of much talent. Her portrait of an elderly lady in white recalls Manet. It has fine qualities, but we much prefer the *Family Group*, which though in oil looks like a pastel, and shows the same lady surrounded by children. Barring its mannerisms this work is beautifully painted." [16]

About this exhibition Rewald observes that Mary Cassatt's "unceasing attempts to interest her countrymen in impressionist art" had played a definite part in keeping the general public from following the views of the more conservative 'connoisseurs.' He adds, "But more important even was the fact that Durand-Ruel was largely known in America as the early defender and dealer of the by then highly popular Barbizon school. This reputation had led the American public to the very realistic conclusion — a conclusion which the French had failed to draw — that since he so consistently supported his new friends, their works ought to have some value. Both critics and visitors thus approached his show without prejudice. 'Don't think that the Americans are savages,' Durand-Ruel wrote to Fantin. 'On the contrary, they are less ignorant, less bound by routine than our French collectors.' " [17]

Looking back from the vantage point of 1958, Germain Bazin, the Conservateur-en-Chef of the Louvre, observed about this exhibition: "The press was divided. The unfavourable notices were, however, much less virulent than in Paris. The 'revolting' aspect of the pictures was much less apparent to the New York journalists than to the Parisians. . . . Generally speaking, however, the press took this demonstration of modern art very seriously. It was welcomed with that cordiality which the Americans always bestow on foreign manifestations in their midst. The fact that it was a commercial undertaking and that the pictures were for sale did not displease them. On the contrary to do business is, in the U.S.A., a good guarantee for the success of any undertaking. The commercial character of any transaction enables it to be taken seriously, and the dealers in works of art are sometimes, in the U.S.A., listened to with more attention than the curators of museums, because they defend the commercial interests of their firms. Durand-Ruel was feted, and the results of the sale, though not spectacular, were very encouraging, 18,000 dollars on a declared value of $86,320, or almost a quarter. . . ." [18]

The following year Mary moved to the apartment and studio she was to keep for the rest of her life. It was at 10 rue Marignan. Near the Champs Elysée, the building was quietly impressive, white and several stories high like so many of the fine structures in that area. Close, wrought-iron balconies decorated the windows. A high iron gate with gilt trimmings opened from the street onto a covered way for carriages. She continued to work in the midst of family life, and her own friends came and went. Huysmans and Zola were not among her visitors, but "they admired her without knowing her personally." [19] Mrs. Potter Palmer of Chicago came under Mary's influence when she was in Paris in 1889. Mrs. Palmer was the wife of one of Chicago's richest and most influential residents and in her own right and opinion the first lady of her city's Society. She was beautiful, charming to everyone and a consummate executive. In due course she was to add to her home, known

as The Palmer Castle, an extensive art gallery. Under the guid-
ing eye of Mary Cassatt she made her first purchase of modern
art: Degas' *On the Stage*.

Mary Cassatt's resourcefulness in seizing such opportunities
as this both to forward the cause of the group and to secure
fine pictures for America did not distract her from her first
responsibility — the constant improvement of her own work.
"Like Manet," wrote Isham, "she sees the world with no desire to alter it to ideal pre-conceptions . . . ." [20] Bettering the
technique for conveying what she saw absorbed her, and her
work showed steady improvement. Segard discusses her continuing growth. "From 1874 her work takes shape, the design
tightens, the drawing becomes more vigorous and more incisive. Miss Cassatt felt her way and she felt her way through
design. To a large extent she controlled a natural quality of
which she herself felt sure and from which she well knew she
would someday draw fine effects: the gift of seeing as a col-
ourist . . . ." [21] Segard adds a warning: "This gift for seeing
with color and enjoying it involves for painters a serious danger. It is a delicious pleasure but it may also be a facile pleasure. To see only the color often means that the painter works
only in a superficial manner . . . . Miss Cassatt well understood
this danger . . . . She entered upon her artistic career with un-
limited respect for the great masters of the past and for the
modern painters whom she recognized as masters. She was
naturally modest. Far from letting herself exploit a facility, a
natural virtuosity, she felt the necessity of pulling herself together, of concentrating, of seeing with discernment, under
the appearance of color, the realities of volume, of movement,
of line and of feeling. Precisely because she was a woman and
naturally inclined toward the pretty and gracious, she gave
herself the severest masters, those best suited to curb her tem-

Courtesy Melvin Gelman Collection
Washington, D.C.
Photograph from Durand-Ruel, Paris

Maternité

perament in so far as it could have been facile and superficial. She knew she must develop her work in design and in
depth . . . ." [22]

An example of the resulting achievement is Mary Cassatt's
pastel, *Maternité*. Owned previously by Ambroise Vollard in
Paris, it was sold in May 1965 at the first trans-Atlantic tele-
vised art auction ever held — relayed by the Early Bird com-
munications satellite. The picture was displayed at Sotheby's
in London, together with a pastel by Degas, a painting by Sir
Winston Churchill, and a number of Audubon prints. The
sale was conducted in London, with bids being made simul-
taneously there and at the Parke-Bernet Galleries in New York.
Mary Cassatt's pastel was purchased by an American for
$35,000.

Chapter IV

THE COLOR PRINTS
AND RELATED WORK

Mary Cassatt, on her way with Degas to the Paris exhibition of Japanese prints in 1890, was moving toward another significant point in her work. Behind her were a series of forward thrusts: her firm confrontation of her father as she announced that she meant to be an artist; her departure for Europe; her steadying into a professional attitude with the ground work of her study of masterpieces; her painting pictures that were accepted by the Paris Salon. Then came the exciting shock of discovering a new kind of painting, her exhilarated sympathy with the new movement under the inspiration of Manet, Degas, Pissarro and others, with consequent release of new power in her own work. As her painting gained in depth and sureness, she knew the feel of her own progress. There was no doubt she was on the right track.

Now in 1890 a woman of forty-six, she had made and kept her own way of working, though her approach had grown and altered, taking strength from any dynamic trend that was congenial to her basic tenets and instinctive feeling. Constantly she studied the old masters, but she did not permit epochs or schools to limit her exploration. When she observed in the canvases of her contemporaries a method, a perception she could adapt to enrich her own work, she eagerly learned what their pictures had to teach her.

To her mature work she also brought something else. This was serenity, and its essence was unaffected by occasional flashes of anger. For Mary Cassatt was one of those women, rare in the nineteenth century, who achieved a vigorous and pleasing harmony within themselves without the experience of marriage. Always she preferred men's society to women's — aside from a few special woman friends — and while this was partly due to their livelier and better-trained minds, she fully enjoyed their delighted response to her innate graciousness and charm. (More than one was especially devoted to her.) She had always wanted to lead a well-rounded life, and the companionship and admiration of men were certainly part of such a life. If art did not absorb so much of her time and interest, she might of course — But, as it was, art *did* possess her. It was true that her wealth and social status gave her wider and more interesting contacts than a less endowed woman might have had. Her dinner parties, in attractive surroundings, were delightful, the food and wine excellent, the service expert. But there was also the contribution of Mary Cassatt as a person. Well-informed, articulate, vigorous in her views and prejudices, she was an inspiring talker. And if the subject was art — as was by no means always the case — she knew about it as observer as well as practitioner, for she had visited the chief art centers of Europe to study the great creations for herself. She knew personally all the contemporary French artists whom she considered important. The one thing she would not talk about in general conversation was her own work. If guests urged her to do so, she evaded them. She suggested another line of interest — Wouldn't they like to see the beautiful

The Fitting

stained glass at Beauvais? She would love to drive them over to look at it.

Meanwhile, what were the qualities and urges that enabled her to live so well-balanced a life? Biddle speaks of her "splendid detachment." How had she evolved a satisfactory perspective on claims for her time and attention? Effortlessly she put her work first — *effortlessly* because she would always rather work than do anything else. But there was one exception to the primacy of work. When her immediate family needed her, there was never any question of denying their claim. To Lydia, to her father and mother, and even to small nephews and nieces, she gave herself completely when they were ill or ailing. When the sieges of sickness were long, she sometimes lamented the lack of time and energy for painting. She never questioned the necessity of helping. And self-pity was as alien to her as false sentiment.

This family exception to work-first was an early sign of a resolution Mary adhered to — that she would live her life as well as she could. During and after the war, when blindness made it impossible for her to paint, she went straight ahead with the business of living each day as it came along. Though her powers weakened with old age, her standards did not. Having asserted her independence at an early age, she had accepted responsibility for her life. It was her job. Though she was objective and detached to a certain degree, she did not hold aloof from what was going on. There was no withdrawal into herself to the neglect of the world. She concentrated on the immediate job, and her resolve to acquit herself well as a person, as well as an artist, supported her. The compelling urges within her seem not to have included any desire to prove postulates of the women's movement of the day. That her professional success and her manner of living did demonstrate the ability of one woman to cope with problems in what was then sometimes called "a man's world" — was to her merely incidental. Nor did she have ambition to achieve fame for herself as a woman aside from being an artist. As her best work shows, she learned to convey universal feeling. She had deliberately worked for this goal, pulling free of limitations of time and place. In her life, as in her art, she cared for sound structure, sure patterns, clear lines, with no superficial prettying-up and no glossing over of the truth. There was also her huge enjoyment in being alive.

Concentrating on her work through long days of painting and etching, Mary Cassatt was yet aware that back home all was not as she would have liked it to be where appreciation of the arts was concerned. It was true that the comments of a few knowledgeable and discriminating people about the Durand-Ruel exhibitions in New York had heartened her. Here and there the press had been more open-minded than she had expected. But all of this was a drop in the bucket compared to the massive indifference of her countrymen to the vital aspect of life that was Art.

In mid-November 1890, a new journal was issued in Paris, *L'Art dans Deux Mondes*. The "two worlds" were France and her native land. There was a short biographic note about herself containing a preliminary observation: "Her works are known by only a small number of artists, and yet she has already attained an important place among the painters of the school of Realism." [1]

This may or may not have pleased her, but her eye was caught immediately by a leading article entitled *"Art en Amérique."* Written from the French point of view it began: "The fashion has not yet passed, even among our artists, of jeering at the Americans . . . ." After giving what might have been considered the view of the man-in-the-street as to what an American was like, the article continued: "One is willing to see in him only the primitive Yankee, enterprising in business and without culture. If he buys beautiful pictures, it is for ostentation. If he seeks well-being and elegance, it is for love of himself. His luxury manifests itself as common display. The book that he prefers is his great book of commerce. What he understands of design is the advantage that a builder or a manufacturer of machines can obtain from it." [2]

Though no American could read such comments without a surge of anger, Mary Cassatt knew there was still some truth behind the indictment even as the nineteenth century drew to a close. Unable because of acute mal-de-mer to cross the Atlantic, except on rare occasions, she nonetheless kept in touch with family and friends. She followed closely national political developments in the United States, and through her interest in investments she knew something of the outlook and attitude of business. Often she heartily wished that things were different, that neither superficial values nor monetary considerations were quite so important to people at home as they seemed to be.

It was heartening to read on: "At such absurd prejudices serious men shrug their shoulders . . . . Our fathers saw the American people acquire the rank of a nation . . . . A hundred years ago America had almost nothing; fifty years ago she began to be something; she plays at present a great role in the world, and everything leads one to believe that in fifty years her power of growth will have no rival . . . . A young nation makes its beginnings by organizing itself. On its organization will depend its future strength . . . . At this first period of existence a people is never artistic. How could it be? Art is a luxury, and luxury has a place only in an advanced civilization. In America during her birth throes it was necessary that there be merchants, manufacturers, planters, bankers, builders and engineers; she did not create poets, painters, musicians nor even tapestry-workers. Everyone arose at dawn and worked until night .... Then one day wealth came. On that day he [the American] feels the desire to travel, to take part in the pleasures of other nations, and the taste for refinements shows itself at once .... From this moment the American has had very marked tendencies toward the arts. He has had architects come from Paris to build his mansions and, without ceasing his own laborious activity, he reveals himself as a collector ....

"But that is not all. As the American civilization has developed, the country has become more and more self-sufficient .... It sends its products abroad .... The barbarous Yankees, taught by us, wish to contribute to our refinement .... This spirit of search, this determined will to find something new which characterize the industrial arts of the United States ought to result, indisputably, in the creation of a national art."[3] With all her heart Mary Cassatt wished it might be so. Twelve years before, she had written to J. Alden Weir: "I always have a hope that at some future time I shall see New York the artist's ground. I think you will create an American School." *

Once Mary wrote a friend about someone's statement that in the evolution of the race, painting was no longer needed. "If painting is no longer needed," she said, "it seems a pity that some of us are born into the world with such a passion for line and color."[4] As Mary entered the Paris Exhibition with Degas, she was to find in the Japanese prints shown there

* *Letter dated March 10, 1878. Reprinted (with permission) in the 1937 catalogue of the Brooklyn Institute of Arts and Sciences Museum.*

an extended horizon for the expression of such a passion in herself.

The last decade of the nineteenth century was to see the culmination of Mary Cassatt's work as an artist. Opening with her visit to the exhibition of Japanese prints, what she saw there made an incisive and lasting impression on both her painting and her graphic work. In the prints of Utamaro, Toyokuni and others she found the beautiful line she loved plus treatment of patterns and color areas that went beyond anything she had encountered before. As with Correggio, Rubens and others of the old masters, as with Courbet, Manet and Degas, she took from Japanese prints only what lent itself to her personal talent.

Nor was this passive acceptance. She brought the force of her imagination and all the vigor of her make-up into this new development of her art. Her dedication to hard work was unceasing. "She imposed on herself a rugged discipline, believing in the value of effort, in difficult work, submitting herself to persistent labor in order to acquire exactitude of touch, the expression of truth, the quality of style that she demanded of herself," said Simone Cammas, Conservateur du Musée Departmental de l'Oise. "She had a constant desire to penetrate the intimate structure of things, and that profound research she imposed on herself through design. She was a designer *hors ligne*. The supremely instructive practice of engraving taught her an incisive, significant, vigorous touch . . . ." [5]

Prints were not in popular demand at the close of the century, but she was far less interested in the market than in trying new approaches and processes that might strengthen her art. Accordingly she set to work on a series of color prints. On the copper plates she applied the color with little balls of twisted rags that she called "poupees." Since each color print required more than one plate, the meticulous matching of these was an operation of extreme precision. She herself pulled the first set of ten color prints from the press. When she had the help of a professional, she acknowledged his aid when she signed them.

By some critics Mary Cassatt's prints have been considered her finest work. Commenting on those made from 1889 to 1899, Adelyn D. Breeskin, the authority on Mary Cassatt's graphic art, writes: "In them we find her main characteristics, such as the originality of vision, the elimination of non-essentials, the arabesque quality of asymmetrical design, the strong linear patterns, as well as the unconventional angle of perspective and well-articulated, rounded forms." And further Mrs. Breeskin states that her color prints are "her most original contribution . . . and, as color prints, have never been surpassed." [6]

Lemoisne speaks of Mary Cassatt's development toward this period: "Between all the early works of Mary Cassatt, between those that she made around 1879 and those of her maturity, we feel a progression regular and sure in her design. It steadily increases in perfection and ends by acquiring an ease and a firmness very far removed from certain rather soft studies of her beginnings. This appears with special strength in the engravings she made around 1891; certain of her etchings at this time, certain engravings in color have a solidity, a freedom, a highly-strung quality which denotes magnificent progress . . . ." [7]

A London comment on the color prints noted: "They date of course from her initial look at Japanese coloured woodblocks, but they are differentiated, it appears, by a more tender acuity. Intentionally they stand somewhat flat, but she developed a most telling aptitude for the untouched expanse of a

single colour. Bounding it would be a crisp line . . . ." [8] Another critic added: ". . . their flatness and the predilection for
stripes and flower ornaments also point ahead, as far as Matisse . . . ." [9] Of an exhibition of her work held long after her
death it was written: "Among the most exciting things shown
were the series of colour prints . . . . Here the juxtaposition of
three prints by Utamaro did not shame the artist; the exotic
treatment of everyday subjects was not only fascinating in itself, but demonstrated effectively her affinity with their sensitivity and simplification of line." [10]

But here again Mary Cassatt was no copyist; here again she
integrated into her own way of working what she learned from
the Japanese. "Miss Cassatt loved the Japanese and she studied them, but she imitated them only in spirit and in truth.
Her imitation is as little literal as possible." [11]

Rewald referring to "Mary Cassatt's ingenious use of the
various techniques" goes on to say: "Combined with her superb draftsmanship, it was her clever and subtle exploitation
of all the possibilities of the media that particularly distinguished her prints. To draw openly acknowledged inspiration
from Japanese woodcuts and yet to achieve a style and a technique entirely her own was not the least of Mary Cassatt's
merits." [12]

Nor was the influence of Japanese prints confined to her
graphic work. *Young Women Picking Fruit* (The Carnegie
Institute, Pittsburgh) was done in the same year her color
prints were made. The Carnegie Institute through its magazine recognized that there was a strong Japanese quality in this
picture — "particularly in the design, flat color pattern, and
the decorative effects . . . . Mary Cassatt treated her space
either in canvas, on prints or on a wall as a decorative problem
and never as a sounding board for propaganda. The theme of

Young Women — is a very simple one. It has wholesomeness, serenity, and a beauty not dependent on sweetness or sentimentality. It was done according to the nature of paint. It is unusual in composition. The two figures in the picture, the one seated and the other standing, and the flower hedge were painted by a keen and sympathetic eye by one who never allowed her subject to stand in the way of artistic and technical considerations. The painting has robustness, vitality, and yet restraint and is without any appeal to the popular liking for prettiness. Here is dignity and repose, and withal strength, vigor and truth." [13]

Pausing before her color print, *Woman Bathing*, Degas said to Mary, "That back, you modeled it?" [14] The answer was No, and Segard explains, "Now in order to obtain that result, the artist did not even need to indicate shadow. That back curves by the sole power of the perfectly executed line. It has subtle precision, the more remarkable since that bit of mastery was obtained directly on copper without a preliminary design." [15]

Gazing at it, Degas was heard to say, "*Je n'admets pas qu'une femme puisse dessiner comme ça.*" ("I do not admit that a woman can draw like that.") Says Lemoisne, "Degas, delighted with her progress, was moreover unstinting in his praise of the series of color prints in which he admired the beauty of the design." [16]

Of all the comments made about her color prints, none would probably have pleased Mary Cassatt, the woman, more than that appearing in the bulletin of the Metropolitan Museum at the time of an exhibition of prints: "The prints of Miss Cassatt are perhaps unique among all the prints that have been made in the world for a very curious and interesting reason. They represent easy, nice, clean people, pleasant women and fat babies, quietly and simply and without any fuss or

Woman Bathing (*Femme à sa toilette*)

nonsense of cooing or other sentimentality of the doting variety. There is no parade of artistry or special techniques. There is the sharp-sighted but detached point of view of one to whom these things are an accepted and necessary part of life. Just as the artist was learned in the traditions of her craft, she was learned in the plain, pleasant facts of family life." [17]

Reviewing the exhibition organized by Frederick A. Sweet in 1954 at the Art Institute of Chicago and then shown at the Metropolitan Museum in New York (*Sargent, Whistler and Mary Cassatt*) a critic wrote: "It was not until 1890 when she was 45, that Cassatt turned to the theme of the mother and child, a theme with which her name is always associated. These paintings exploit all that is most observant and precise in a draftsmanship of impeccable skill, in a radiant use of color, particularly in the flesh areas, and in a point of view which is full of tenderness and comprehension but without sentimentality or overemphasis." [18]

About the time of her work on color prints, Mary was painting the *Mother and Child* (The Wichita Art Museum), a painting "any museum in the world would be proud of," as a commentator observed. "Mary Cassatt's most telling device was her own: she painted plain and sometimes charmless people in classically noble poses, and with the same care that earlier artists lavished on saints and goddesses. Cool-headed and warm-hearted, easy and austere, her art had the perfect balance that only will-power achieves. Beyond that, Painter Cassatt was blessed with psychological penetration as unwelcome in the Victorian age as it is prized today . . . ." [19]

Reservations about her work were also expressed. "What robs her of the important rank to which her vigorous style ought to entitle her is a lack of individuality of mind . . . ."

Mother and Child

wrote Richardson. "She offers us a circumscribed Jamesian world of well-bred ladies living lives of leisure, delighting in their dresses, their company and their well-behaved children. There is an odd contrast between the boldness of her style and the world of perpetual afternoon tea it serves to record. Did she exhaust her sense of discovery in becoming an artist at all? ('I would rather see you dead,' said her father.) For all its distinction, her art is that of a very conventional person living in the very conventional world of the 'nineties. As a recorder of the female side of that little circle of wealth and privilege, she will always have a place. But — tea, clothes and nursery; nursery, clothes and tea." [20]

Mary Cassatt used what she knew, and the limited area of her subjects mattered less to her because she attached paramount importance to line, structure, pattern and color. Perhaps also she listened to her friend Degas who no doubt said to her what he wrote to Bartholomé: "But it is essential to do the same subject over and over again, ten times, a hundred times . . . ." [21]

Degas continued as counselor and friend in the peak years of Mary's achievement, though not all his attention was focused on her work. Now and then he persuaded her to pose for him. Mary made a good model both because she was observant and adaptable and also because she had extensive experience in dealing with models herself. For many of her paintings she prevailed on members of her family to pose. When the Cassatt household were spending a summer at Marly-le-Roi, Mary's mother wrote one of her granddaughters ". . . your Aunt Mary counts on painting out of doors and wishes she had you all there to put in her pictures. Do you remember the one she painted of you and Rob and Elsie listening to me reading fairy tales? She finished it after you

left and it is now at the exhibition. A gentleman wants to buy
it but I don't think your Aunt Mary will sell it. She could
hardly sell her mother and nieces and nephews, I think."

In using relatives as models Mary no doubt experienced
difficulties similar to the ones Degas described when he went
to visit his brothers in New Orleans. "Nothing is as difficult
as doing family portraits," he wrote Tissot. "To make a cousin
sit for you who is feeding an imp of two months is quite hard
work. To get young children to pose on the steps is another
job of work which doubles the fatigues of the first...." [22]
And to a Danish painter friend: "The family portraits, they
have to be done more or less to suit the family taste, by impossible lighting, very much disturbed, with models full of
affection but a little *sans-gêne* and taking you far less seriously
because you are their nephew or their cousin. I have just
messed up a large pastel and am somewhat mortified." [23]

On one occasion, when Mary was doing a portrait of two
small nieces, their mother tried to keep them quiet by reading
Huckleberry Finn. This proved a dubious procedure, however,
for Mary laughed so much herself she could not paint and had
to ask her sister-in-law to stop.

Mary's friend, George Moore, once observed that "absorption in the model is perhaps the first quality in portrait painting." [24] While giving due heed to the model, Mary was usually
objective as far as the person before her was concerned. No
matter how devoted she might be to the individuals who sat
for her, they became, as she painted, the properties of her art.
It was the picture as an entity that mattered to her, and this
feeling overshadowed for the most part exact representation.
Her objective view did not, however, exclude a certain psychological penetration which "while remaining discreet and rather
aristocratic, was full of insight." [25]

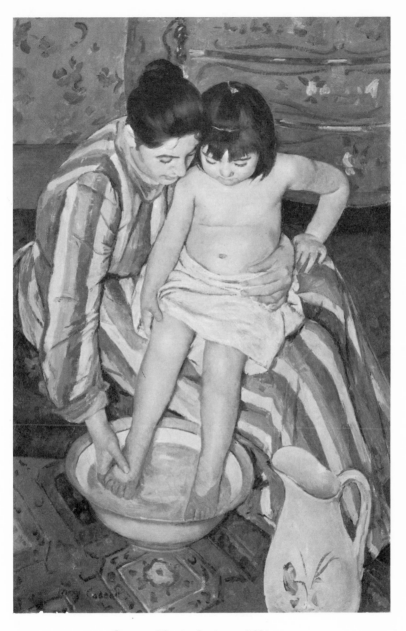

The Bath (*La toilette*)

With the model before her she was selective. Segard speaks of this quality of hers with regard to costume: "The artist painted always from the model, alive and clothed in the style of her period, but she chose little by little from these stylish costumes what would be characteristic and consequently time-less, in order to avoid instinctively those exaggerations of dress which, in a little while, cease to be interesting and become ridiculous." [26]

She also used her neighbors as models. One day she wrote to Minnie, "I have a model of eleven months old who is a wonder. To keep the cover straight on the floor (he is standing on it) I had a six-pound weight placed there. He leans down and lifts it. Isn't that very remarkable for an eleven-month baby? I think it must be. I hope Alexander isn't such an ath-lete. I think it too much."

Though Degas kept an eye on his younger American friend, he occasionally stole time from his criticism of her work and from his own painting for other esthetic pleasures. In addition to writing charming letters when he was in the mood, he tried his hand at poetry. His friend, the poet Stéphane Mallarmé, whom he saw frequently at Mary's home, encouraged him. Degas was interested in his hostess' pet parrot, Coco, and one day composed a sonnet in its honor; this he dedicated "A Mademoiselle Cassatt à propos de son Coco chéri."

PERROQUET

Quand cette voix criait, presque humaine, là-bas,
Au long commencement d'une même journée,
Ou durant qu'il lisait sur sa Bible fanée,
Que devait ressentir ce Robinson si las?

Cette voix de la bête, a lui accoutumée,
Le faisait-elle rire? Au moins, il ne dit pas
S'il en pleurait, le pauvre. A cris perçants et gras
Elle allait le nommant dans son île fermée.

C'est vous qui le plaignez, non pas lui qui vous plaint;
Le vôtre ... Mais sachez, comme un tout petit saint,
Qu'un Coco se recueille et débite en sa fuite

Ce qu'a dit votre cœur, au confident ouvert,
Avec le bout de l'aile, enlevez-lui de suite
Un bout de langue, alors, il est muet ... et vert.

Degas was aware also of his friend's devotion to dogs and wrote his friend, Le Comte Lepic, who was not only a painter and engraver but a great dog breeder: "Could you not either from your kennels and apartments, or from your friends and acquaintances, find me a small griffon, thoroughbred or not (dog or bitch) and send it to me to Paris if an opportunity arises or by carrier.... I think it in good taste to warn you that the person who desires this dog is Mlle Cassatt, that she approached me, who am known for the quality of my dogs and for my affection for them as for my old friends etc. etc. I also think that it is useless to give you any information about the asker whom you know for a good painter, at this moment engrossed in the study of the reflection and shadow of chairs and dresses, for which she has the greatest affection and understanding.... This distinguished person whose friendship I honour, as you would in my place, asked me to recommend to you the youth of the subject. It is a young dog that she needs, so that he may love her." [27]

Chapter V

THE ONE-MAN SHOWS; PANELS FOR CHICAGO

At last in 1891 Mary Cassatt felt ready for a one-man show. It was held at Durand-Ruel's gallery at the same time as the exhibition of the Société des Peintres-Graveurs Français. The Société had decided earlier in the year to limit its showings to French citizens. This of course excluded Mary, and since she had exhibited with them up to this time she was unhappy about the change in their rules. It also excluded Pissarro, born in the West Indies and hence a Danish subject. Mary was especially sorry about this, for she knew Pissarro was experiencing unusually hard times just then. She had tried to aid him in various ways. On one occasion she wrote asking if he would be willing to give lessons to three American girls. He replied he would be glad to have them visit him but could make no charge. To help the sale of his paintings, she often showed them to her guests and she sent prospective buyers to his studio, as she did to the studios of other painters.

Convinced of the high quality of Pissarro's work, it distressed her to see him in dire straits for lack of buyers. He was the personification of despair when he could not buy the necessities of life for his wife and children. His seizures of gloom were, however, relatively brief — perhaps of shorter duration than the family's deprivations — for his philosophy rescued him. "Painting, art in general, enchants me," he wrote his son Lucien from Rouen one November day. "It is my life. What else matters? When you put all your soul into a work, all that is noble in you, you cannot fail to find a kindred soul who understands you. You do not need a host of such spirits. Is not that all an artist should wish for?" [1]

Now that they were both excluded from the Société, she suggested to him that he show along with her at the Durand-Ruel gallery. It was accordingly arranged that he should have twelve etchings, as well as drawings, pastels and gouaches — twenty-four things in all, in one room, while she exhibited the same number in another.

Following the show she wrote to Durand-Ruel telling him of two inquiries about her work that had come to her from prospective purchasers. "I replied both to Mr. Hirsch and to M. Brigeau that I had no power to sell them any proofs as the etchings were no longer my property. Only as M. Brigeau wrote me so very polite a note, I would ask your permission to give him a proof, or ask you rather to sell him one. I only thought that the etchings not having sold in America . . . were left on your hands." Apparently Durand-Ruel was finding more purchasers for Mary Cassatt's etchings in France than he had in the United States, for she added, "I am very glad you have any sale for them in Paris. Of course it is more flattering from an Art point of view than if they are sold in America. But I am still very much disappointed that my compatriots have so little liking for any of my work." [2]

When Mrs. Potter Palmer, wealthy social leader of Chicago, came to Paris she had not only consulted Mary about the pur-

Courtesy Collection Mr. Richman Proskauer, New York
Photograph by Brenwasser, New York

Self Portrait

chase of a Degas painting but had evidently been much impressed with Mary Cassatt's own work. In 1891 Mrs. Palmer was made chairman of the Board of Lady Managers for the Columbia Exposition. The following year she asked Mary to do the panels for one end of the main gallery in the Women's Building. It was Mary Cassatt's first commission in America. She undertook it with pleasure and seriousness.

Immediately there were technical difficulties. The canvases had to be very large. Mary decided that instead of standing on a ladder to work at the top of the paintings, she would have an excavation made and lower the canvas into it. Then there was a mix-up in the mailing of contracts, and when Mary's finally reached her it was wholly unsatisfactory. At once she cabled Mrs. Palmer: "Contract received, conditions impossible, if maintained I must resign." Evidently the paramount condition was that she send the authorities preliminary plans for her proposed work. Feeling that such procedure would tie her hands in an undertaking that must evolve during the creative process, she would have none of it. Writing a friend at the same time she said, "I see by your letter that the stumbling block will be my not sending a sketch, and as I don't know why they should make an exception in my favor, I will wait a few days for Mrs. Palmer's answer to my cable and then resign . . . . I am very sorry for all this misunderstanding, but now that I am thrown off the track, I hardly feel as if I could get back onto it again." [3]

There was delay also in sending her the exact dimensions. In an appreciative letter of thanks to Mrs. Palmer for her help in smoothing out difficulties with the board of construction, Mary observed: "Between you and me I hardly think women could be more unbusinesslike than some of the men are. Here is Mr. . . . sending me 'the exact size of those tympana' at this hour of the day! It will entail on me a good deal of extra work which he might just as well have spared me by sending the exact size at first. However," she added, "it would be ungracious to grumble for really I have enjoyed this new experience in art immensely and am infinitely obliged to you for the opportunity you have given me. All I could wish would be a little more time; I am afraid my work will show signs of hurry, and it would have been better if we could have had two long summers instead of one." She added further, "And as if by a 'fait expres' all my relatives seem to have given each other rendezvous in Paris this summer and one cannot exactly refuse to see them." [4]

In early September Mary's sister-in-law wrote her son Eddie: "Aunt Mary has contracted for those three huge panels for the World's Fair. She must get them done before Christmas ... and proposes to stay out until she finishes them. *Entre nous*, she will not be through before the first of March. I think they will freeze out there. It is a great undertaking and I hope she will do something which will be a credit to herself and to you all and to her country. She has models staying there and she bought the dresses for the picture from the best dressmakers in Paris."

When in place the panels would be at a great height, "about the fourth floor of the large apartment houses in Paris," Mary thought. She continued, in a letter to the wife of the Exhibition sculptor, "I had the 'rentoileur' of the Musée du Louvre here the other day; he thinks it will be impossible to place the decorations otherwise than on stretchers on account of the rounding top which would make it impossible to stretch properly on a flat wall." [5]

In early October Mary Cassatt wrote Mrs. Palmer about how she hoped to carry out her idea of the decoration. "Mr.

Avery sent me an article from one of the New York papers this summer in which the writer, referring to the order given me, said my subject was to be the 'Modern Woman as glorified by Worth'! That would hardly describe my idea, of course. I have tried to express the modern woman in the fashions of our day and I have tried to represent those fashions as accurately and as much in detail as possible. I took for the subject of the central and largest composition young women plucking the fruits of knowledge or science — That enabled me to place my figures out of doors and allowed of brilliancy of color. I have tried to make the general effect as bright, as gay, as amusing as possible. The occasion is one of rejoicing: a great National fête. I reserved all the seriousness for the execution, for the drawing and painting. My ideal would have been one of those admirable old tapestries brilliant yet soft. My figures are rather under life size although they seem as large as life. I could not imagine women in modern dress eight or more feet high. — An American friend asked me in rather a huffy tone the other day, 'Then this is woman apart from her relations to man?' I told him it was. Men, I have no doubt, are painted in all their vigor on the walls of the other buildings; to us the sweetness of childhood, the charm of womanhood — if I have not conveyed some sense of that charm, in one word if I have not been absolutely feminine, then I have failed. My central canvas I hope to finish in a few days. . . . I think, my dear Mrs. Palmer, that if you were here and I could take you out to my studio and show you what I have done that you would be pleased. Indeed without too much vanity, I may say I am almost sure you would. When the work reaches Chicago, when it is dragged up 48 feet and you will have to stretch your neck to get sight of it at all, whether you will like it then, is another question . . . ." [6]

On December first she received a cable from Mrs. Palmer and replied at once. "I am infinitely obliged to you for the kind thought which prompted you to send it. The fact is I am beginning to feel the strain a little and am apt to get a little blue and despondent. Your cable came just at the right moment to act as a stimulant. I have been shut up here so long now with one idea, that I am no longer capable of judging what I have done. I have been half a dozen times on the point of asking Degas to come and see my work, but if he happens to be in the mood he would demolish me so completely that I could never pick myself up in time to finish for the exhibition. Still he is the only man I know whose judgment would be a help to me — Mr. Durand-Ruel, poor man, was here with his daughter a week ago. It was most kind of him to come. They are all broken-hearted over the death of poor Charles. M. Durand was very kind and encouraging, said he would buy it if it were for sale, and of course from his point of view that was very complimentary but it was not what I wanted. He seemed to be amazed at my thinking it necessary to strive for a high degree of finish; but I found that he had never seen the frescoes of the early Italian Masters . . . . I have one of the sides well under way and I hope to have the whole finished in time for you to have it up and out of the way by the end of February." [7]

The panels were finished, duly shipped, and mounted high in the main gallery. Since the Exposition they have not been seen. Perhaps they were demolished with the building.

Mary Cassatt's second one-man exhibition at Durand-Ruel's gallery in 1893 was well received by several of her colleagues. Pissarro wrote his son: "At this moment Miss Cassatt has a very impressive show at Durand-Ruel's. She is really very able." [8]

There were also a number of press notices.* About the family-circle pictures it was said: "These are scenes a thousand times seen, but no painter has seen them with so much feeling nor has anyone with such convincing art translated onto canvas the poem of the family. One comes away from that exhibition with a fine impression of serenity and of harmony which strikes all visitors. Mlle Mary Cassatt has already exhibited at the Salon du Champ-de-Mars. Here she achieves the most lively success.

"Her aquatints are of extraordinary design and exquisite taste. They by themselves alone deserve long study."

There was also reference to "Miss Cassatt who possesses along with the most exquisite gifts of color and design, that rare quality among women artists of genuine individuality . . . . there is also a penetrating and fine feminine feeling, a way of seeing and expressing as a woman, but as a woman who, according to the apt expression of La Bruyère, 'has all the qualities of an honest man.' "

Referring to Miss Cassatt's "superb exposition" another of the reviews continued: "What strikes one in this remarkable collection is the sound workmanship, the job knowledgeably carried through, the supple and virile design, the masculine palette, if I may thus express myself. For the art of Mary Cassatt has a feminine inclination only in the subjects that she treats. It is Woman that she paints, but rarely the elegant, the coquettish or the frivolous woman: it is the mother of a family busy with daily tasks and especially with care for her child.

---

* *Subsequent quotations are from the volume in the Durand-Ruel library in Paris entitled* Coupures de Journaux 1892-1907, France-Étranger.

Portrait of Mme. Aude and her Two Daughters

(Madame Aude was a sister of the three Durand-Ruel brothers who were
Mary Cassatt's dealers. The family were her close friends.)

She treats this eternal subject — maternity — with the most subtle talent and without resorting to preraphaelist means as false as they would have been out of place . . . .

"We all recognize Miss Cassatt's models: they breathe the air that gives us life and her painting moves us because she speaks to the heart. Gifted with an exceptional temperament the artist makes light of technical difficulties and color is displayed in her pictures with a masterly skill that reminds us of Manet, Renoir and her master and friend, Degas.

"Miss Cassatt — woman of the world — most certainly does not condescend to paint exact portraits. Certain spectators at the theatre have served her as pretexts for the study of light, atmosphere, rich materials, shimmering irresistible colors but she returns always to the 'mamans et aux bébés' of which she has made herself the artist." Later there is reference in the review to an etching made "with the searching look of a Daumier."

In the opinion of another reviewer: ". . . Still very feminine in her choice of subjects, the art of Miss Cassatt is extremely virile in execution. This is not painting effete or involved or delicate to excess as is the work of so many Parisians to whom the gallantry of the juries opens wide the doors of the expositions. It is something younger, more simple and, especially, infinitely more bracing . . . .

"It must be said in all sincerity, as one of my colleagues has written, 'Miss Cassatt is perhaps, beside Whistler, the only artist of high talent, personable and distinguished, whom America actually possesses.' That opinion seems to me completely justified."

This same year (1893) Mary Cassatt had the pleasure of meeting the Whittemores of Naugatuck, Connecticut. Mr. Whittemore was in Europe the first part of the year, and they

Child in a Straw Hat

became good friends. When Mary visited them in America, she made three family portraits in pastel.

Back in Europe, Mary replied to a letter from Mr. Whittemore: ". . . It is delightful to me that you should want another of my pictures in the future. If I do anything I think particularly successful I will let you know . . . . I have an interesting piece of artistic news for you. There was in Paris an amateur by name de Bellio, who had a large collection of Monets, Pissarros, one or two Manets, Degas, one, I believe; the Renoirs and Monets very fine. This man has died lately and it is most probable that his collection will be sold . . . . I remember your wanting to buy some good Renoirs, this will be a chance; in the collection was a picture by Monet, which he called 'An Impression.' It was taken up by the papers and was the origin of the name 'Impressionist.' My brother offered Mr. de Bellio 5000 frs for it eleven years ago. That was a high price then but he was refused. As soon as I have any more particulars I will send them to you." [9]

Business conditions in America and in France at this time were hard on painters. "The dealers are transfixed by the bad turn things have taken in America and here," wrote Pissarro. "They can't make a penny." [10] And some eight months later: "Just conceive that the collectors in Paris are so dismayed by events that they won't hear art spoken of now; in America it is even worse, nothing, nothing! . . . Miss Cassatt says it is simply due to the election and that the situation will be restored when the new group comes in! . . ." [11] Meanwhile Mary urged Pissarro to show his etchings with her in New York. He declined — "I am working on paintings at the moment, I don't want to lose my good mood; and then if I go in for that sort of thing, goodbye to painting in the open which Degas ridicules so wittily." [12]

During the Dreyfus affair, Mary and her friend Degas sharply disagreed, for Degas was what Pissarro called "the ferocious anti-Semite." [13] There was special reason at this time for Degas' petulance. His sight was steadily growing poorer. Trouble with his eyes was not a new difficulty. Long ago when he had enlisted in the infantry during the Franco-Prussian War he was found to be almost blind in one eye. Now his vision was increasingly impaired. Though he kept working, he referred to "this filthy studio to which love of glory binds me." [14] With Eugene Manet and Rouart he helped arrange a posthumous exhibition of the works of Berthe Morisot. To Henri Rouart he wrote in the spring and summer of 1896: "I have not done badly, without much progress. Everything is long for a blind man, who wants to pretend that he can see." And sending congratulations on the birth of a child, added, "During my cold, I am meditating on the state of celibacy, and a good three-quarters of what I tell myself is sad." [15]

"For my part I prefer the valley of the Oise," Mary had once remarked. It was gentle, friendly country with broad stretches of sunlit farming land. Not far from Beauvais in Le Mesnil-Théribus (Oise) she finally found a chateau to her taste. It was Beaufresne, a large house with some forty acres of land and magnificent trees. She bought it with satisfaction and began making improvements. Indoors she liked especially the oval dining room. A mirror in the ceiling reflected lamps and candles. Outdoors a brook from a spring in the walled vegetable garden fed a pond. She had the pond stocked with California trout because she liked their colors. When these grew to edible size, her guests often fished for their luncheons. Strawberries and asparagus were among the products of her garden; she had tomatoes and eggplant grown under glass.

But even with these luxuries the Cassatts missed the food they had been accustomed to at home — canvasbacks, turkeys, cranberries, terrapin. In the winters which they spent in Paris, Aleck sent them packages to add variety to their meals: "oysters as fresh as if eaten in Philadelphia . . . . The ducks seem in perfect condition . . . sweet potatoes better than those of last year — quite dry and sweet." Once Mrs. Cassatt wrote her son: "The hams are the nicest I ever saw . . . . The apples are perfect. Mary who hasn't tasted an American apple for years, begrudges everyone I give away and when we tell her that she has found at last something better in America than here she says, 'Oh I never denied that the living was far better at home than here.' "

Beaufresne was a long, narrow house built about 1690. Much renovation was needed, and Mary went about this eagerly. It was her aim to make Beaufresne eminently comfortable as well as attractive. Though her father had died two years before she moved into her permanent country home, her mother enjoyed many months at Beaufresne before her death in 1895. In memory of her family Mary had erected a beautiful simple monument in the village cemetery:

Sépulture de la Famille

CASSATT

native de Pennsylvanie
États-Unis de l'Amérique

Here in due course were buried her brother, Robert Kelso Cassatt, who had died at Darmstadt when he was twelve, her sister Lydia, her father and mother and later Mary Cassatt herself.

The first spring of the new century found Mary rejoicing in her country residence. Writing to a friend about how absorbing and exciting she would find a new house to be, Mary spoke about Beaufresne: "I know what I felt when getting settled here, how I fretted to get the workmen away and then only to call them back again, and I have been doing nothing else ever since. I rather flatter myself you would not know Beaufresne again. I have done more plumbing, another bathroom, etc. I hope I am now nearly up to the American standard. I need not say that I am so far beyond my French neighbors that they think I am demented. Mrs. Havemeyer sent me a book on gardening, 'The English flower garden etc,' which I told her would be my ruin, and now that my lawns have all been properly turned over and levelled and walks designed and made I have gone into roses, and every day I bend carefully over my delicate 'teas' to watch the shoots. I have over a thousand planted and already fancy myself sniffing the perfume and revelling in the color. Oh! you will enjoy your place. There is nothing like making pictures with real things." [16]

Chapter VI

TO ITALY, SICILY AND SPAIN

In 1901 Mary Cassatt accompanied the Havemeyers on a tour of Italy, Sicily and Spain — a picture-buying tour. Mr. Havemeyer was determined to build a fine collection, and he was often to rely on Miss Cassatt as his consultant.

Mary's judgment had already led friends to invest in the Impressionists and other contemporary painters. Now here was an opportunity to use her critical skill in wider fields. It has been said that if she had never painted a picture of her own, she would deserve to be included in art history because of all she did to secure paintings for the United States through acting as consultant to American collectors.[1] Never to leave her was the recollection of her own early days when lack of masterpieces in America had compelled her to pull up roots and go abroad to study.

She was a good executive. Like her brother Aleck, president of the Pennsylvania Railroad, she was able to get things done, to make her aims materialize. So when she received an invitation from Mr. Havemeyer to go with him and his wife on their journey, she gave thought to what such a trip might be made to yield in addition to her own great pleasure in it. Here was

Courtesy Collection of Mr. and Mrs. Dunbar Bostwick
Shelburne, Vermont
Photograph from Durand-Ruel, Paris

Mrs. Havemeyer and her Daughter Electra

the large Havemeyer fortune, here were interest in the arts and a desire to possess fine pictures, here was her own influence which she might extend to guide selection.

Years before, she had advised Mrs. Havemeyer — then Louisine Waldron Elder — in the buying of her first picture. She had urged her to purchase a Degas pastel. "The pastel was a *Répétition de Ballet*," Mrs. Havemeyer wrote later. "Old Plugue, the well-known *maître de ballet*, stood leaning upon his stick by the side scenes of the stage directing a rehearsal, the dancers were grouped about in various poses awaiting their turn while a *première* did a difficult *pas seul* in the foreground. The drawing of the picture was as firm as a primitive, the difficulties of planes and perspective handled like a master, while the effect of light and shade and the beauty of color were simply entrancing. It was so new and strange to me! I scarcely knew how to appreciate it, or whether I liked it or not, for I believe it takes special brain cells to understand Degas. There was nothing the matter with Miss Cassatt's brain cells, however, and she left me in no doubt as to the desirability of the purchase and I bought it upon her advice . . . ." [2]

Mary was genuinely attached to the Havemeyers. Mrs. Havemeyer had become one of her dearest friends. Travel with them on a picture-buying journey would be delightful. She was of a mind to enjoy it to the full.

They were to meet her in Genoa. They sailed into the harbor "after a miserable night," wrote Mrs. Havemeyer, "and in the bright sunlight of early morning, from the upper deck I could see Miss Cassatt walking impatiently up and down the wharf . . . ." *

---

* *The account of this trip, unless otherwise indicated, is based on Mrs. Havemeyer's book*, Sixteen to Sixty, Memoirs of a Collector. *Privately printed for the family of Mrs. H. O. Havemeyer and the Metropolitan Museum of Art, New York, it is copyrighted by the Metropolitan Museum, 1961.*

Impatiently — Ahead lay a new adventure for Mary: strengthening in Mr. Havemeyer his growing interest in possessing art, and locating pictures for him to possess. "As the French say," wrote Mrs. Havemeyer, "Miss Cassatt had the 'flair' of an old hunter, and her experience had made her as patient as Job and as wise as Solomon in art matters; Mr. Havemeyer had the true energy of a collector, while I — well, I had the time of my life."

So they were off with Mrs. Havemeyer's sister as the fourth member of the party. After Turin, Mary persuaded them to go to Milan to see the Luinis, the Veroneses and the Moronis. She was anxious they should have a Moroni in their collection. They visited all the dealers and found one fairly good Moroni, but Mary convinced Mr. Havemeyer that it was not up to his standard, so they did not buy it.

Sicily was their next objective, and since Mary suffered even more than Mrs. Havemeyer from seasickness, they went by train to Reggio and crossed the Straits to Messina. They were enraptured by the place. "Of all the colonies in Sicily," wrote Mrs. Havemeyer, "I believe the Greeks must have loved Taormina best, and here they built their loveliest theater." When they entered it and looked off to the far horizon Mary exclaimed, "Didn't they know how to build? What a background for a play!"

When they arrived in Palermo, Mary and Mrs. Havemeyer entertained their companions with accounts of "the great Roger of Sicily and his fair Juliana" as Lenormant had described them and their brilliant court life. They knew the three volumes of *La Grande Grèce* almost by heart. "It is the last word on travels and ought to be translated into every language," said Miss Cassatt. "Did you know it inspired George Gissing's *By the Ionian Sea*?"

On their return they spent a day at Reggio waiting for the night train to Naples, and while their two companions made themselves comfortable before a bright fire in the hotel, Mary and Mrs. Havemeyer went in search of old glass and old rings. They also walked down to the shore, where they could see Mount Etna across the Straits and again recalled Lenormant. Mary asked her friend if she remembered his description of the Calabrian earthquake in 1663. "What a description that was! The best I ever read," she said. "It seems those who lived through it never smiled again. Do you recall the poor man who was caught among the falling timbers of his house, and they robbed him, while still alive, of the silver buckles off his shoes as his feet stuck out between the beams?"

From Naples, toward the end of February, Mary sent a letter to Durand-Ruel. "I could not write you from Genoa nor since for I have not had a minute to myself. We have travelled very fast, one day to each city so far. Mr. Havemeyer very much wants a Velasquez which he will certainly not be able to get in Rome, nor elsewhere in Italy. I have told him that you will inquire in England and with this he has been well satisfied. A Velasquez of the first quality for himself and for a friend is what he dreams most about." It was then Mr. Havemeyer's plan to return to Paris before going on to Spain, and it was Mary's hope that when they went through Paris, Durand-Ruel would have something to offer him. "We have had atrocious weather, snow and unbelievable cold . . . ." [3]

On the train to Rome both Mary and Mrs. Havemeyer were carsick and utterly miserable. But at Rome they pulled themselves together and went to see Veronese's *Europa*. Mr. Havemeyer was so taken with it that eventually four Veroneses were secured for their gallery. They also determined to see all the Domenichinos in Rome. "Degas admires Domenichino so

much," said Mary, "and wonders he is so little known." Then
she abruptly remarked, "It upsets me terribly to see all this art.
It will be months before I can settle down to work again!"

As they arrived in Florence Mrs. Havemeyer echoed Mary's
complaints about the weather: "Cold, snow, frost, ice and
wind!" It took willpower to leave what heat there was in the
hotel. But presently Mary and Mr. Havemeyer ventured forth
to visit a large dealer. There they saw a salesman whom Mary
had known slightly when she had lived in Italy. "He was an
artist then, doing small things, *putti*, etc., and seemed rather
successful." Subsequently hard times had overtaken him. With
his Italian wife he came to see the travellers and eventually
he was made the Havemeyers' agent. He led them into various
picture-hunting adventures, which intrigued Mrs. Havemeyer
especially, and in the long run they bought a number of pictures through his instrumentality.

Returning then to Paris, they settled Mrs. Havemeyer's sister comfortably in Mary's apartment and presently the other
three set out for Madrid and the Prado. "Mr. Havemeyer always maintained," his wife wrote, "that after the Spanish War
we should have demanded the Prado as an indemnity instead
of taking over the Philippines."

It was at the Prado that the Havemeyers encountered El
Greco, a painter little known outside Spain at that time. With
swift decision Mr. Havemeyer wanted to possess an El Greco,
and one morning soon after, Mary announced to him that his
wife and she were going in search of one. He seemed pleased
and said they had better add a Goya while they were about it.

"Perhaps we may, who knows?" replied Mary Cassatt.

First they bought a photograph of every El Greco and every
Goya they could find. Then they went to see Señor Cossio,
who was writing the life of Greco and compiling a catalogue

of his works. After this they walked up four flights of stairs to an apartment where a woman showed them two portraits of her ancestor, "La doña Zárate," painted by Goya. Carried away by the beauty of the paintings, Mary made a mistake, as she acknowledged to Mrs. Havemeyer later as they went back down the stairs. She had offered twenty-thousand pesetas for the two pictures — an offer the owner flatly refused. "I should not have made such an offer," said Mary disgusted with herself. "Now she will ask five times as much." Sure enough — that evening a note was brought to them at their hotel saying the owner would part with the pair of Goyas for one hundred thousand pesetas. The Havemeyers refused the offer. Years later Mrs. Havemeyer saw one of the Zárates at a dealer's priced at forty-five thousand dollars.

But their morning was not yet over. As they went back toward their hotel, they passed an "antiquity" shop, and Mary noticed a picture placed in the doorway. "There he is," she cried. "That Christ there, that small picture. It is Greco surely. No one else could have done those hands. Look!"

They went over and examined the painting carefully. At last Mary said, "Yes, my dear. That is a Greco, or I am mistaken, and a fine one. Do you suppose they are so plentiful they can be found like this?"

In French Mrs. Havemeyer asked the price. The dealer replied in Spanish. Mrs. Havemeyer did not understand Spanish, but she assumed the price was too high, shook her head and turned to go. This gesture released a flood of Spanish from the dealer, and Mary, recalling some of the Spanish she had once known, completed the transaction. The Greco was Mrs. Havemeyer's for a little more than two hundred and fifty dollars. She carried it away under her arm.

When the Havemeyers decided to make a special trip to the

south of Spain, Mary pleaded excuses and remained in Madrid. She said she was going often to the Prado while they were away. Her chief reason for staying, however, was to search for an El Greco for Mr. Havemeyer. She was successful. When they returned — "Knowing Miss Cassatt would be expecting us, we returned to Madrid and to the Puerta del Sol with a sense of homecoming" — she told them she had met the Infanta's godson who spoke English and knew where fine pictures were to be found.

"Does he know where to find a Greco?" demanded Mr. Havemeyer.

"Yes, I have seen one, a magnificent portrait by Greco, a full-length seated portrait of a cardinal in splendid red robes. I believe he had something to do with the Inquisition, and he has let fall a letter he has just been reading; he wears huge tortoise-shell spectacles as they did in those days."

"Spectacles in a portrait? I would not consider it! They must be terrible."

"No, they look perfectly natural. A great painter knows how to preserve the relation of things. You forget the spectacles and see only the glance of the eyes. Besides," she added, "you know very well a man of the cardinal's age could not read without glasses."

But Mr. Havemeyer would not consider such a picture. He asked what else she had found. She told him her new Spanish acquaintance had also taken her to see a landscape by Greco, a view of Toledo. Both pictures were there in Madrid, and her adviser thought that if she and the Havemeyers kept in the background he could manage in time to get both of them. Mary had also asked about a Goya she remembered having seen many years before when she was in Spain — some women on a balcony. Mrs. Havemeyer's account continues: "He knew

where it was and we went to see it; it took us all day. When
we arrived at the place we found the picture had been stored
away, but W. [their adviser] managed to have several cases
opened and I saw the Goya and another Greco, a huge altar-
piece, the *Assumption of the Virgin*. It is perfectly splendid in
color; I think it must be an early work for it is so Venetian
in style and composition."

Three years later the Goya thus found was theirs. "*Las
Majas al Balcón* for some reason went to Paris," Mrs. Havemeyer recorded, "and remained a while with Miss Cassatt and
was greatly admired by the critics who dropped into her apartment to see it. When she finally shipped it to us she wrote:
'Roger Marx congratulates you on the possession of this Goya
which he considers very fine, and says it is extraordinary for
Goya to paint the women's faces as if they were miniatures.' " [4]

The Havemeyers purchased also a *Portrait of Wellington*
by Goya (The National Gallery of Art, Washington) and
El Greco's *View of Toledo* (The Metropolitan Museum of
Art, New York).

The Infanta's godson was killed in a hunting accident the
following year, and so it was Durand-Ruel who went to Spain
to complete negotiations for several purchases by Mr. Havemeyer, including Greco's *Assumption of the Virgin*, which
Mary Cassatt had "unearthed that day in the Bourbon Palace." [5] The latter was so large, however, that it posed a problem. ". . . when I learned," explains Mrs. Havemeyer, "that the
picture measured fifteen feet without the frame, I knew it
would be an impossibility to hang it properly in our gallery
and I asked my husband's permission to offer it to our Metropolitan Museum." [6] The Metropolitan had, however, acquired
another El Greco and declined the opportunity to buy it at
the original purchase price. Mrs. Havemeyer was greatly disap-

pointed and wrote at once to Mary Cassatt. Mary promptly communicated with the Art Institute of Chicago, where the picture now hangs.

Meanwhile the Havemeyers, while still in Spain, had a chance to buy a Patinir "for the indefatigable Miss Cassatt had more than one string to her bow in hunting for pictures." She explained to Mr. Havemeyer that since his wife had so often spoken of Patinir she thought she might like to possess one. "It is certainly very fine."

Mrs. Havemeyer describes the arrival at their hotel of a pale, sickly little man carrying a canvas. He unwrapped his package "and sure enough I saw a beautiful example of that early Flemish master. The bright green, the conventional background so wonderfully drawn, the clear atmosphere and the still life were done with such perfection as only the followers of Van Eyck were able to do it; a charming Madonna, naive even in her gorgeous dress, held the infant Jesus upon her knee . . . . The little owner knelt as he told us all about it and showed us exactly where the tiny altar lamp had done some damage to the picture which had been deftly restored. He seemed very modest about its beauty and its worth." The price was about thirty-four hundred dollars. It was the first time they had had to decide about a fifteenth-century painting, and they felt somewhat at a loss, for Mary admitted she had never seen a Patinir before. "Why, let us go to the Prado," she said suddenly. "There must be one there."

There proved to be not one but two fine examples of this painter's work, and they presently decided that the one offered them was worth the price.

When at last they were preparing to leave Madrid, their Spanish adviser came to say goodbye to them. Mrs. Havemeyer remarked that if he found any Hispano-Moresque plates not to let them pass. The Spaniard was surprised and said if he had known she was interested in such plates he could have taken her to a palace where she could have bought them off the walls, for their owners needed money badly.

"Why not go now?" asked Mary.

They estimated the time before their train was scheduled to leave for Paris and thought they could make it. Mr. Havemeyer declined to go along, but admonished them not to miss the train. Then to their amazement he said abruptly, "And go get your old cardinal with the glasses."

Mrs. Havemeyer records: "We looked at him incredulously, but I knew he was again, as he had done many times before, only deferring to Miss Cassatt's sound judgment."

The Cardinal (*Cardinal Don Fernando Niño de Guevara*) by El Greco is now in the Metropolitan Museum in New York as part of the Havemeyer Collection.

Chapter VII

BEGINNING OF THE NEW CENTURY

Mary Cassatt was in her mid-fifties at the beginning of the century. She said art was her life, and she must have felt satisfaction that she had already achieved such a body of work.
Common sense told her that she had not received in her own
country the recognition her painting deserved. She knew also
that even in France, where the value of her work was more
fully accepted, she did not have the reputation a French
woman would have had in her place. She was aware of falling
between two stools, being foreign-born in the land of her
achievement and being an expatriate to most of her fellow
countrymen. She felt also that her acceptance as an artist was
circumscribed by her being a woman. There is no evidence of
bitterness about these facts. They were merely, for her, facets
of the total situation.

   Though her temper was often quick to flare, and though
the artist in her longed for understanding and recognition in
proportion to her achievement, she had one reason for special
thankfulness as the new century moved forward. She had had
time to show what she could do before her eyes failed her.
For this she was grateful. And even in the early nineteen-hun-
dreds her eyes did not seriously interfere with her work,

though she was too honest to hide from herself that her working time was limited. Characteristically she accepted what could not be altered. She would not lower her standards. She continued to paint as well as she could, to live her non-professional life with dignity, to be gracious to her guests and warmly understanding of her family.

In August 1902, *L'Art Décoratif* carried a substantial article about her by Camille Mauclair: "Un Peintre de l'Enfance, Miss Mary Cassatt." Her enthusiasm, as she began reading it, was reserved at first, while the author elaborated the differences between children and adults. Clearly what he was trying to say could be conveyed more felicitously in paint or pastel — unless one were a poet. Toward the end of the second page she was mentioned for the first time, but didn't it rub the bloom off a painter's creation to spell it out? "Miss Mary Cassatt is perhaps the only painter of this time who has given the child an interpretation limited to himself: she is not impatient, before that being-in-formation, to divine his maturity. She arrests her tranquil and sure contemplation at the very moment when the creature being studied appears before her, she seizes the present individuality, and that suffices to her to create a new psychology, captivating and strongly inspired by nature."

Then he went on to compare her with others who had painted children: "The infants of Eugène Carrière are overwhelmed with precocious thoughts: across their tender heads shines the phosphorescent light of the mind . . . their expressions are unfathomably serious . . . these are the messengers of the race of tomorrow, and a melancholy maturity wearies them, that divine and mysterious fatigue already wandering over the faces of Velasquez's children. The children of Renoir and of Besnard are only flowers and fruits; of a delicate animal life they live only by the efflorescence of their downy flesh, the freshness of which is not yet impregnated with the essence of perception. The young girls of Mlle Breslau are animated by a nervous life; their eyes are shrewd, their movements already reserved and stylized by education. They have for their first thought obedience to charming good manners. Other painters strive to sketch the adult through the child or, if they show him at an early age, wailing and almost shapeless, they undertake to suggest through him all the mysterious terror of non-being; they evoke in this larva the life pre-organic; if they endow him with a soul, it is too elderly or it is the spring of spiritism.

"Miss Cassatt has had the rare merit of observing the child's individuality in its first phase, from two to three years, and of showing it neither anticipating nor informed. She does this by the strength of her painter's observation that does not separate the flesh from the spirit, and she owes her success in this difficult study to her admirable pictorial sincerity that resorts to no intellectual artifice. She makes a painting and nothing more, she represents what she sees; she makes use neither of the stratagem of shadow nor of decoration nor of allegory . . . . with the children that she paints, the soul has the exact age of the bony structure and of the nervous system . . . ."

Farther along in the article she found that he called her "one of the foremost pastellists of the times." A later critic was to enlarge on this: "That she can build up a rounded form out of a multitude of straight strokes is one of the recurrent wonders of her technical method. Always we are conscious of the kinship of her viewpoint with pastel as a medium." [1] She paused in her reading to recall her visits to Saint-Quentin to study the work of the great eighteenth-century pastellist, La Tour. Amazing what that man had been able to do! Such brilliancy of color, such grace and such obvious delight in his work. The beautiful pictures moved across her memory — gorgeous blues, sparkling highlights. Incredible master.

But she must finish the article. "It would be puerile to set oneself to compare Miss Cassatt with other women painters exhibiting in our epoch, and to estimate her qualities in relation to those of Eva Gonzalès, Berthe Morisot, Louise Breslau, Marie Duhem, Cecilia Beaux, Hélène Dufau, Nancy Adam, Mary Schwob or several other women who hold high rank among modern painters. Such superfluous comparisons would appear to admit, by useless restrictions, that there exists a demarcation between men and women in an art where the latter have for all time shown its non-existence. Miss Cassatt shows by her work that virile qualities are not incompatible with femininity: there are in her infantile scenes movements that only a woman would observe, understand and transcribe and these she has executed with such truth that her canvases will endure . . . ."

This was kind of M. Mauclair. Her eye travelled on. Yes, he was certainly right that there were many complications in creating a "simple" picture. On the whole, the article gratified her. It had penetration and more understanding than one might have hoped for.

Meanwhile Mary Cassatt enjoyed her everyday life, whether in her Paris apartment or at her chateau in the Oise valley. After all she felt life to be an entity even when it included both professional and non-professional life. She had always seen it whole, though there had been a firm line between what she did as an artist and the rest of her activities. Whether in town or at Beaufresne she had frequent guests — the Havemeyers, of course, and the Durand-Ruels; young people from

America and many relatives. Always interested in the young, whether related to her or not, she not only welcomed them into her home, but arranged amusements for them, including luncheon parties and evenings at the theatre. "I remember her so well as she first came to greet me," wrote a young American. "She wore a flowing sort of gown with ruffles and ribbons" and several small dogs "were jumping about her feet and playing with the ribbons." [2]

Distinguished work was to come from her studio during the dozen years or so before the First World War. Nonetheless her fierce dedication to her own development had eased. It was as though she knew her abilities had reached maturity, as though she knew she had pushed her talent as far as it would go. From this self-knowledge, whether then fully recognized or not, had sprung her decision to stop work for a while and go with the Havemeyers on their long picture-buying journey. She returned to work, and she would continue working rigorously, enjoying it, but the drive toward new creative effort — such as the color prints — had diminished in force. Though quite promptly back on the rails of professional labor after her travels, the heights were behind her. Breeskin puts it this way: "At its best there is a quality of great austerity and of deep seriousness in her work. Now [after 1900] there was added a lighter touch, a rhythmic ease born partly of confidence but also reflecting less of the profound essence of her personality and character." [3] George Biddle went farther: "Miss Cassatt was almost unaware of anything that happened in the world of art after 1910." [4] Camille Mauclair had remarked earlier: "What she has done no one has done in the same way: she has controlled her originality by her great, her serious love of sincere work, with a happily accurate sense of her exact destination and of the natural limits of her temperament and of her art." [5]

Increasingly her eyes troubled her. Increasingly also she was concerned about her family, as though she needed them now more than ever. Neither of these anxieties, however, lessened her interest in what was going on in the world beyond art and family. "The other day I had a visit from M. Clemenceau, now a Senator," she wrote home in the early spring of 1903. "He is quite a power again, after having been under a cloud for so long." In the summer of 1904 she expressed concern about the Presidential elections at home. "Any number of Americans are over here . . . . We are much interested in the elections. I think it is about time there was a change of party in power . . . ."

When Theodore Roosevelt in the summer of 1905 was exerting all the authority he could summon to negotiate a settlement of the Russo-Japanese War, Mary wrote to one of her family: "It makes me shiver to read the description of the Portsmouth weather with those four peace envoys almost obliged to flee before the mosquitoes. However the Russians must be used to them and the Japs too. According to the 'Herald', the Russians have all the sympathy at home and if it is shown so plainly as that horrid paper pretends, I fear the Japs must think us rude, to say the least . . . ."

The following spring she broke off a report of recent guests in Paris to remark: "On Thursday we had a sort of black fog all morning, the result of the Vesuvius eruption. It seemed impossible the dust and smoke could travel so far." Early in 1907 her personal plans were disrupted, due — indirectly — to strenuous activities in the United States. "I expected to join the Havemeyers in Spain in March, but Mr. Havemeyer is too busy repulsing the attacks on the Sugar Trust to leave home . . . ." The close of the same year finds her increasingly concerned about economic conditions in America. A friend had written about the bad times there. "Surely," Mary protested in a letter to Minnie,* "people not in business cannot have been entirely ruined as she says was the case with some who crossed on the same boat with them, and who from wealth are in direst poverty, living in two rooms in a poor part of New York! The suicides one sees in the papers are appalling . . . . Our friends the Germans are not so admiring of our strenuous president as they were before they lost money on American securities."

When her nephew Rob joined her brother Gard at the bank, Mary was delighted. To Minnie she wrote: "I told him when you were over here that he was on the road to be a millionaire. Now he will have to learn the 'metier' and take to collecting or libraries! I hope not the latter."

Meanwhile Americans continued to consult her about buying pictures. To a member of the board of the Philadelphia Museum of Art she wrote from Paris in reply to a request from him: "I gave your name to M. Joseph Durand-Ruel with a request that he would facilitate your efforts to see Manet's and Degas' pictures so if you will see him when you go to the rue Lafitte he will tell you what can be done. Faure, the famous baritone of the Opera and friend of Manet's, has still some fine pictures of his, and also some of Degas though he sold his finest Degas to —— in New York; you see everything is fast coming our way, unfortunately not yet to our public galleries. Several people must disappear before we can hope for any change there . . . .

"Please believe that I will do all in my power to help you.

* *Minnie was the wife of Aleck's son, Robert, and so Mary Cassatt's niece by marriage.*

I have lived so long in the intimacy of artists now so celebrated, but, when I first knew them, so neglected, and as far as Degas is concerned I know so well the sort of advice he gave, I feel it my duty to pass it on."

As she made Beaufresne more and more her home, she became increasingly involved with neighbors and with community affairs. To many of the villagers, whom she helped in various and inconspicuous ways, and to others who respected her high standards in civic affairs, she became the grand lady of the chateau.

An early painting, which she had signed "Mary Stevenson," as she had her first Salon picture, she gave as a wedding present to Martha, her femme-de-chambre, upon her marriage in 1907 to Heinrich Rohrich.*

Chambermaids might come and go, but it was Mathilde who continued to be Mary's standby as she had been to Mrs. Cassatt. The young people in the family called her "Taudy." She managed the household, as well as serving as Mary's personal maid — helping her with her bath as she grew older, dressing her hair, taking care of her clothes. Increasingly she served also as companion, and in the months before Mary's death, stood by the head of her bed when people called and, if words suddenly failed her mistress, quietly supplied them or, when Mary's mind momentarily wandered, reminded her what they were talking about.[6]

Mary Cassatt was always strict, in a reasonable way, with those who served her. No doubt she remembered her father's example when she was a little girl. As his carriage was brought

---

* Long after Mary Cassatt's death it was found in Germany by Karl Loevenich, who has kindly supplied the above data. He adds that after being cleaned two other signatures appeared at the lower left corner, "one partly obliterated, Mary Cassatt." The picture is now owned by the Montclair Art Museum.

around to the front door of their Philadelphia home, he would pull on white cotton gloves, then smooth the shining coats of his horses. If the gloves showed a trace of soil, he would send the equipage back to the stables for more careful grooming. Years later, when her mother and father were living with her in Paris, it became necessary to dispense with the services of their current chef. "We gave him eight days warning this morning," Mary wrote Aleck's wife, "as he adds on to his bills too heavily. Otherwise he is a decent man and a very good cook. I told him that tradespeople did not give commissions to the servants in America, but it seems that Louis, Aleck's man, told him that they had begun to do so in New York. I hope it is not true."

One who served Mary indirectly, by helping Aleck's family, was Mathilde's sister, Bertha. In recommending her, Mary wrote Lois, "She is a thoroughly reliable woman, an excellent lady's maid, dresses hair very well and is a good milliner. She also makes dresses and sews well. At her present place she is a sort of housekeeper, overlooks everything, does all the preserving and she speaks better French than Mathilde and excellent *Italian* besides *Arabic*."

Until Mr. Havemeyer's death, Mary continued to act as their adviser on the purchase of paintings. "How would you like to have a portrait of Clemenceau by Manet?" she asked them one morning when they were visiting her in Paris.* They asked if they might see it.

"Certainly. I saw Clemenceau yesterday and he wants to sell his portrait. He says he does not like it but I rather think he is hard up and wants some money. He really asks very little

* *In the subsequent episodes the material is again drawn from Mrs. Havemeyer's Memoirs.*

for it, only ten thousand francs. The picture is not completely finished, as you may imagine, with the combination of two such men as Clemenceau and Manet. Manet did not finish the still life in the picture, but he had forty sittings for Clemenceau's portrait and I think it is a very fine and interesting picture."

Mrs. Havemeyer continues the account, revealing not only the purchase itself but Mary Cassatt's lively interest in public affairs: "We were soon at Clemenceau's home, a pretty villa out of the whirl of Paris, with an attractive garden, where we found the fearless statesman on whose broad shoulders had fallen the burden of premiership . . . . As if indifferent to the portrait, or the sale of it, he began talking to Miss Cassatt. The subject of their conversation was, of course, politics; church and state, I think, but I was not familiar enough with the proposed 'séparation' to be able to recall intelligently what they said. I do remember that when that subject was rending France, there was a luncheon arranged in the rue Marignan * and Clemenceau met a French minister there, and that through the indiscretion of a priest to whom some papers and letters had been confided, Miss Cassatt's name seemed about to be drawn into the political quarrel, when Clemenceau in a brilliant article written to the papers averted from her the unpleasant notoriety by mentioning that the luncheon was given 'at the home of a lady whose art was one of the glories of France.'

"When Clemenceau and Miss Cassatt had agreed or disagreed — it is sometimes hard to tell the result of a discussion in politics — we returned to the subject of the portrait and we bought it for ten thousand francs, the price at which Clemenceau said he would sell it." [7]

* *Mary Cassatt's residence in Paris.*

The dealer Portier told them later of another portrait by Manet that he thought might be bought at a price. "It's a wonderful portrait of a very ugly man." When Mary learned that it was the portrait of George Moore she said, "Let us see it by all means." Mrs. Havemeyer continues the account: "While we drove to a distant part of Paris . . . Miss Cassatt told us of George Moore and of Manet's painting the portrait. 'George Moore,' she said, 'painted a little. He went to his friends, he even boasted to me, that Manet had invited him to come work in his studio. I was surprised at Manet's doing such a thing but when I saw the portrait I understood it all. While George Moore was studying in Manet's studio, Manet was studying George Moore and painting a portrait of him, and it is one of the finest portraits he ever did. He did George Moore for all time,' said Miss Cassatt. 'Of course George Moore did not like it and said horrid things about it to me . . . .' We looked at it long and silently, then Mr. Havemeyer turned suddenly toward Portier and said, 'You say it is dear? How much do they ask for it?'

" 'Ten thousand francs,' replied Portier with a doleful shake of his head.

" 'We will take it,' said Mr. Havemeyer decidedly . . . ." Mrs. Havemeyer adds, "If it is any consolation, George Moore may know that his portrait attracted more attention than any Manet in our gallery . . . ." [8] (It is now in the Metropolitan Museum.)

When the Havemeyers were in Paris, Degas' studio was of course a focal point of interest to them. Usually Mary went along when they visited him. Mrs. Havemeyer records her own impression: "I thought him a dignified-looking man of medium height, a compact figure, well dressed, rather dark and with fine eyes. There was nothing of the artist *négligé* about him; on the contrary he rather impressed me as a man of the world . . . ." As for his studio no one was allowed to touch the pictures and in places the dust lay thick ". . . . His mother's wedding dress was kept in the top of an old piano that was never opened, and the moths had eaten their way into the very entrails of the horse which had served him as a model when he did his now famous *Race Horses and Jockeys*. That studio was a storehouse of art, for Degas was an indefatigable worker and he had lived in the same workshop for many and many decades, leading as Miss Cassatt has told me, the life of a hermit in its simplicity and frugality, extravagant only when he could find a pastel by La Tour whom he greatly admired, or an Ingres drawing . . . . I believe that only a few of his admirers were at any time welcome to his quiet apartment. On rare occasions he invited a few friends and a foe or two to a dinner which usually consisted of a beefsteak pie, his *pièce de résistance,* while over the feast he threw the *sauce piquante — très piquante —* of his caustic wit which frequently burned deep and hurt hard." [9]

Mrs. Havemeyer also mentions a special occasion at his studio: "I recall one visit to the rue Lavalle, when after we had looked at several pastels lately finished, Degas opened a portfolio to show us some of his drawings. What treasures he revealed! Such immense talent and such endless labor! . . . Degas tenderly lifted the drawings one by one and showed them to us. We could see how greatly he prized them . . . . Mr. Havemeyer requested Degas to let him have some of them but he seemed reluctant to give them up, unable to part with a single one of them. Miss Cassatt took up one drawing and called my husband's attention to it. It was the sketch for *Les Danseuses à la Barre*. It was done upon pink paper and the pen-

ciled squares could still be seen across the figure of the young
ballet girl who grasped the bar and extended her leg in a difficult attitude. It was a superb drawing and Degas watched
us as we admired it. Suddenly he selected two others, signed
them all and handed them to Mr. Havemeyer. We realized
we were the fortunate possessors, not only of his best drawings, but of those he wished us to have. No word of price was
spoken. It was a solemn moment and all details had to be
arranged by our kind intermediary, Miss Cassatt." [10]

At another time, Degas sold the Havemeyers a small oil,
The Designer of Prints, for a thousand dollars. "He asked to
keep it for a time as he wished to add a few touches. He kept
it nearly two years and then told Miss Cassatt he would not
give it up for less than three thousand dollars, as his pictures
during those two years had advanced in price. In vain Miss
Cassatt argued that he had sold the picture for one thousand
dollars to Mr. Havemeyer and that he could not change the
price. It was of no use! Degas was quite stubborn about it,
and the idea was so fixed in his mind that he was entitled to
the increase in value that at last Mr. Havemeyer yielded . . . ."
Mrs. Havemeyer observes that this transaction "cost Degas
Miss Cassatt's friendship for a long time." [11]

Another view of Degas emerges when Mrs. Havemeyer describes the day she discovered in a little vitrine in his studio
the wax figure of his celebrated statue, *La Danseuse.* When
she called his attention to it, "it seemed to awaken pleasant
memories and he became animated and began an interesting
conversation with Miss Cassatt about the past, snapping side-
lights upon the work of his contemporaries and making personal allusions which I did not understand but which greatly
amused Miss Cassatt. It is a great pity she did not keep his
letters, nor write down her impressions of Degas; no one un-

derstood him better...." [12] And she quotes Mary Cassatt as
saying, "He is a philosopher, and there it is."

Though the Havemeyers were to purchase more of his paintings through dealers, their final Degas purchase came about
through Mary's interest and involved two paintings. Of the
first Mary wrote: "It is much in the style of a Vermeer and
quite as interesting, very quiet and reposeful. It is a beautiful
picture. A woman in black seated upon a sofa against the light,
the model was a sister of Berthe Morisot, not handsome, but
a Degas! The picture has never been shown .... Then there
is another thing I am to see, another picture, small, danseuses,
very fine in execution." The next mail brought further description: "The little picture was brought here this morning.
It is no larger than this full sheet of paper .... It is a real tour
de force. When Degas saw it, he turned away and said, 'When
I did that I had my eyes!' ..." [13]

Mrs. Havemeyer was enchanted with both the paintings.
About the little one she wrote: ". . . a small panel about twelve
by seven inches — that's all. But what does it represent — a
large foyer, a room with windows and doors. In the center of
it stands a long mirror, such as is used for ballet rehearsals,
and a grand piano in front of which and leaning his back
against it sits the white-haired violinist with his instrument
under his chin, looking at the ballerina who is taking a step
before the mirror. Upon the polished floor he has placed his
violin case and his high hat into which he has tucked his roll
of music. The inevitable sprinkler stands under the closed
piano and in the room are no less than twelve ballet girls,
stretching their limbs at the *barre*, practicing difficult postures,
adjusting their sandals or leaning against the piano. And as if
not content with the difficulties he had encountered, Degas
paints the reflection of at least two ballerinas in different poses

in the mirror! Think of it! Do you wonder that Degas turned sadly away from the picture and said, 'I had my eyes when I did that.' " (The picture is now in the Metropolitan Museum in New York.)

Honors were now being conferred on Mary Cassatt, but she did not wish to accept them. She refused the Lippincott Prize at the Philadelphia Academy of the Fine Arts and the Harris Prize at Chicago. Regarding the reasons for her refusals she wrote about the latter: "I have received your very kind letter of November 19th telling me of the honor that has been paid to me by the award of the ... Harris prize. Of course I am very much gratified that a picture by me should have been awarded this honor, but it has been given to me through a misunderstanding. The pictures belong to Messieurs Durand-Ruel and were loaned by them under the proviso that they were not to be in competition for any awards. I was one of the original 'Independents' who founded a society where there was to be no jury, no medals, no awards. This was in protest against the government salon and amongst the artists were Monet, Degas, Pissarro, Mme Morisot, Sisley etc. This was in 1879 and since then none of us have sent to any official exhibitions, and have stuck to the original tenets. You see therefore that it is impossible for me to accept what has been so flatteringly offered me. In Philadelphia last year the same honor was offered me, but that also was on account of an error of the Durand-Ruels and I explained it to the Directors as I am doing now. Of course unless you had lived in Paris and seen the ill effects of official exhibitions you can hardly understand how strongly we felt about being 'Independents.' ... Do believe though that I feel highly honored and that I am very grateful for your kindness, first in writing to me about how my pictures were hung and now for your kind note of congratulation." [14]

Nor would Mary Cassatt serve on juries to judge artists' work. Declining one such invitation, she wrote to a fellow-American: "It is a matter of principle with me. I disapprove of the system which in France has always kept out of exhibitions the most original painters. To mention only a few who were victims of the jury system: Corot, Courbet, and Manet had their pictures constantly refused. The last two appealed to the public at one of the Great Exhibitions having at their own expense put up pavilions to house their work .... I regret that we in America have copied the faults over here, here where they are trying to remedy things, too late for the great artists who suffered injustice all their lives .... You see I feel very strongly on this subject and could never bring myself to prevent even the humblest of painters from showing his work ...." [15]

Meanwhile Beaufresne was a delight to her. "I hope you are settled in the country," she wrote to Minnie from Paris in early spring, "and I cannot wish you anything better than the weather we are having. It is even too warm and bright and everything bursting into bud and already the tender green leaves out. I was at Beaufresne last week for the day and felt homesick for the country." Soon she was there. Usually there was a severe water shortage in the summer, but in 1903 there was abundant rainfall "and everywhere else it has been a continuous downpour. I began to wonder why my cistern did not fill when I discovered it leaked." Subsequently she had the cistern enlarged and "a sort of filter put in so that the water may be pure."

The drought was back the following summer. "Such a

Château de Beaufresne. Mary Cassatt's country home
Le Mesnil-Théribus (Oise)

month of July! The heat exceeded anything ever before recorded, and the drought has been terrible." To Minnie she wrote: "I am glad to know that you are to spend the summer by the sea. I almost wish that I were going too, for in this dry climate one longs so for the sight of water. My springs were running and the pond was fast filling and all looked so well here when the dry, usual summer began and now the water is disappearing and in two weeks I will have a mud ditch . . . . I am asking the people who were coming out for the day to come at once before the place is again hideous, without water."

One early fall she wrote to Minnie: "I am now painting with my models in the boat and I sitting on the edge of the water, and in these warm still September days it is lovely; the trout leaping for flies and when we are still we can see them gliding along. The whole beauty of the place is the water. One of my neighbors who has had a stream and dam like mine, told me they had fished a trout and when it was opened found a mole in its stomach. Voracious as they are, I had not thought that possible." And one early October she wrote home: "The poor dear roses are trying their best to bloom amidst the cold, gloomy air. It seems almost unbelievable that it is so early in the fall. It is all so green and bright and the atmosphere of December . . . . the corn is excellent and as I have become a vegetarian I indulge twice a day."

Soon she was telling Minnie: "I suppose I will come to the 'auto' before long, but I don't like the motion." Even so, the Havemeyers thought she should have one and presented her with a Renault limousine. It was then a problem to get someone to drive it. "I left my auto in the country," she remarked at one point, "intending to put Pierre [her coachman] at the manufactory to learn but have, on the advice of friends, engaged another man to teach him the few things he doesn't yet know." When her brother Gardner visited her they set off by motor on rather an extensive expedition. "*Never* was there such a trip . . . the chauffeur lost pounds, and my English boy had to go to the rescue twice. We never mention the machine now — but one thing is certain: it *can't* blow up, even when the boiler, or rather the radiator, cracked. This of course is a doubtful advantage." On another occasion she reported from Beaufresne to Minnie: "I got out here Friday in an hour and forty minutes at the rate of 50 kilometers an hour and so shaken up over these bad roads that I ached all over the next day. That boy was racing a fifty horse-power and did not listen to my remonstrances any more than a graven image. He is just like the chauffeur in *Man and Superman,* if you know the play."

The letters Mary Cassatt wrote her nephew Rob and his wife leave no doubt about her devotion to them. On one occasion when Minnie's mother was returning home from France, Mary sent along "a little Christmas souvenir which you must use for my sake. It is a little gold bowl, Directoire or Louis XVI, I don't know which, for bonbons at the theatre, or stamps on your writing table." And once, in reply to a letter from Minnie, she wrote: "You don't know how I appreciate your caring to get letters from me." When their first son, Alexander J. Cassatt, was born Mary was delighted that the Cassatt name would be carried on. She replied at once to Rob's cable: "I am more pleased that you have a boy in your generation, and I fancy his grandfather [Aleck] must be enchanted. I hope you had not too hard a time, and that you will soon be well. Of course I want to know who he looks like, what color his eyes are, and also his name. I am so superstitious I did not send the baby a present before his arrival. I wanted to know him safe here but he will get a dozen of the

Kelso spoons as soon as I can have them made." Kelso was a frequently recurring name in the Cassatt family, and with her gift young Alexander would become the seventh generation to possess spoons made in the old design. Presently she went to England to make arrangements to have the spoons made. "Oh such a crossing! I was carried on shore at Dover, and was so sick for hours after landing that Mathilde could not get me undressed until midnight . . . . I don't think I will try England again." But she was able to report that the Kelso spoons, in the old English shape, would eventually be ready though it would take some time to copy them "on account of the crest in relief."

As her letters home reveal, Mary Cassatt was very much a family person. It was she who looked after her sister and her parents when they were ill. And after Lydia's death it was she who served as companion as well as nurse to her mother and father as they grew older. Through the ups and downs of family illnesses she kept her brothers posted. When she was left alone in France after her mother's death, she continued to write frequently. In the summer of 1906 she grew more and more concerned about Aleck's health. The death of his daughter Katharine had been a terrible blow to him both directly and because it nearly prostrated his wife. Also economic affairs in America were difficult at this time for men in large businesses such as the Pennsylvania Railroad. "Mr. Stillman said to me," Mary wrote Minnie, "that my brother had helped to make the country, and in any other country, especially in England, he would be surrounded with respect in his declining years, while with us they only wished to pull him down." She then added with emphasis: "Of course our 'illustrious President,' as they call him over here, is much in fault. I think though that the sensible ones even here are beginning to think him a demagogue." Mary was concerned about the load Aleck was carrying and expressed to Minnie the hope that all his worries would not make him ill.

Whatever the cause, Aleck did become ill and then, in his sister's view, went back to work too soon. "I am so anxious that I find it very hard to stay here and go on with my work . . . ." Then in a postscript: "How I envy people who can go and come over that ocean and not be a wreck after it!"

There was a bright spot in the news when the Robert Cassatts' second son, Anthony, was born. Mary was pleased. "I do hope your boy will have as good health and as long a life as his great-grandfather born a hundred years ago. His grandfather must be delighted. It ought to make him well again."

Three days after Christmas, 1906, Aleck died. To Minnie Mary wrote a couple of months later: "It is of course selfish to want to keep one's own here if it is to suffer, yet one cannot help missing them dreadfully. I feel as if a force had gone out of my life and left me so much weaker."

She went on to say she had a picture she thought Rob might like to have, "a portrait of his Father done at Marly and very like what he was in those days. The picture was never finished but the head and shoulders are, which is the important part. Elsie when she was a child thought it was her father sitting on the floor, so you see it was a likeness. If Rob, when he sees it, thinks it is I will give it to him. Last summer a dealer came out and rummaged in the garret at Beaufresne carrying off a lot of canvases, and I burned the rest, but kept this portrait, too good to destroy, and which I would not like anyone but Rob to have."

Within the year after Aleck's death, Mary and her brother Gardner made a special trip to Darmstadt where their brother

Portrait of Alexander J. Cassatt
(Mary Cassatt's brother "Aleck")

Robert Kelso Cassatt was buried. To Rob she wrote soon after their return to Beaufresne: "It is settled that I will go there before the end of the year and bring with me all there is left. I am to have a permit to pass everything at the frontier, and no examinations. In one way I felt as if I did not care to disturb the grave, and the cemetery is one of the most beautiful in Germany, but I know it is best that everyone should be here where I can leave money for keeping all in order."

Sad and lonely though she was, Mary kept at work. She also developed her role as adviser to American collectors. She wrote to Durand-Ruel in the Havemeyers' behalf about a head of Degas' and about two Goyas. If the price was too high for Mr. Havemeyer she would urge Mrs. Havemeyer to persuade a friend to buy them. Other possible purchasers were mentioned in her correspondence including one Monsieur Lawrence who told her that to complete his collection of her pictures he still needed two more but of less grandeur than those she ordinarily made. She told Durand-Ruel she would be willing to have M. Lawrence have the picture of the young woman with a child in her arms. "I believe you have sent it to New York." [16]

She was also glad to be told by Durand-Ruel that her last pictures pleased M. Degas. "He is sometimes kind even to excess." [17]

During this period, Mary Cassatt's work was being exhibited not only in Paris, in London and in Manchester, but also in the United States in such cities as Buffalo, Chicago, Cincinnati, Indianapolis, Minneapolis, New York City, Philadelphia, Pittsburgh, Portland (Oregon), Providence, Richmond (Indiana), Washington and Worcester. In the autumn before her last trip to America she sent Durand-Ruel a list of the paintings and pastels she would like shown in their November

3-28, 1908, exhibition of her work — provided people then owning them were willing to loan them.

Mary had contact also with other dealers. In his *Recollections of a Picture Dealer*, Ambroise Vollard suddenly exclaims: "Mary Cassatt! At the time of my first attempts, when I used to ask myself anxiously what the morrow would be like, how often did she get me providentially out of a difficulty!

" 'Have you a picture for the Havemeyers?'

"It was with a sort of frenzy that generous Mary Cassatt laboured for the success of her comrades: Monet, Pissarro, Cézanne, Sisley and the rest. But what indifference where her own painting was concerned! What an aversion for 'pushing' her work in public. One day at an exhibition, they were fighting for and against the Impressionists. 'But,' said someone, speaking to Mary Cassatt without knowing who she was, 'you are forgetting a foreign painter that Degas ranks very high.'

" 'Who is that?' she asked in astonishment.

" 'Mary Cassatt.'

"Without false modesty, quite naturally, she exclaimed, 'Oh nonsense!'

" 'She is jealous,' murmured the other, turning away." [18]

In November 1908, Durand-Ruel did hold an exhibition of her work in Paris. The *New York Herald* (Paris edition) for November 5 referred to her as "the fine and celebrated American artist whose talents, at once robust and delicate, the general public has had only rare opportunities for admiring." Mary was interested also to read the further comment: "Yet if her works are known to only a small number they do not deserve less admiration and their place is among the first of the *école du vrai* . . . . For a number of years Mary Cassatt has held a very high and undisputed place among the moderns. Characteristically she has always clearly avoided any subjection to a formula alien to her own vision as well as all compromise, devoting her life to art for art's sake . . . ."

Early in the century, Mary Cassatt was made Chevalier of the Legion of Honor. Commenting on this, M. Clemenceau told her he did not need to see the ribbon to know she was a great painter.[19]

Chapter VIII

THE HALF-DOZEN YEARS BEFORE
WORLD WAR I

Something of the shock and grief Mary Cassatt experienced in her brother's death now befell her friend, Mrs. Havemeyer. Suddenly, in December 1907, her husband died. Mary wanted to go to her at once but, in the then state of her health, the doctor would not permit a winter crossing. To Minnie she wrote: "I lose in Mr. Havemeyer a friend and am sincerely grieved but of course any feeling I have is swallowed up in sympathy for her . . . . she is sad and broken."

In the spring Mrs. Havemeyer and her daughter, Electra, came to France. Mary met them and did all in her power to comfort her friend. She even agreed to visit Mrs. Havemeyer in America, and when the time came stoically kept her promise and made her last crossing of the Atlantic.

In her friend's New York home she gradually recovered from severe seasickness. When she was better, she wrote Minnie relaying an invitation from her hostess to come with Rob for lunch. Mrs. Havemeyer wanted them to see her pictures and to meet her daughter, Mrs. Frelinghuysen. "I wish Alexander could come with you." Then in conclusion, "We have any number of engagements of course but I am well enough now to enjoy it." Perhaps she remembered fleetingly how little she had enjoyed the press notice of her earlier visit to America: *Mary Cassatt, sister of Mr. Cassatt, president of the Pennsylvania Railroad, returned from Europe yesterday. She has been studying painting in France and owns the smallest Pekingese dog in the world.*

Visiting friends and relatives, she found herself occasionally invited to a type of entertainment unknown in her life in France — a large luncheon for ladies. After several of these experiences, she inquired whether the men never ate lunch in Philadelphia.[1] Spending so much of her life in France with men, she missed them in America. Perhaps it occurred to her to wonder how the artists she knew so well regarded her — an American and a woman. Renoir's son says his father liked Mary Cassatt very much "though as a rule he did not care much for women painters — 'except Berthe Morisot, so feminine she would make Raphael's *Virgin with the Rabbit* jealous.' On one of his painting trips he had met Mary Cassatt in Brittany. 'She carried her easel like a man.'"[2] Pissarro considered her his friend, liked her as a person and admired her as an artist. Degas said he would not admit a woman could draw so well, and then appropriated for his own collection the picture he was referring to. A young American wrote of her that she was always a woman painter, never a lady painter.[3] Gauguin considered Berthe Morisot and Mary Cassatt and then said: "Miss Cassatt has as much charm and more force."[4]

How aware Mary was of these views is not known, but it is probable, absorbed in her work as she was, that she considered her colleagues primarily as fellow-artists and when she was away from Paris missed her daily contacts with them and the stimulating professional talk.

Back in France after her American sojourn, life went on

much as usual for a while. She wrote Durand-Ruel for the name of the director of the Moroni Gallery at Bergamo. She had mislaid it and wanted to send him a letter introducing a young American painter. She also inquired about a certain portrait by Franz Hals. Was it available? What would be the price? Mrs. Havemeyer's son "very much wants a Hals." [5]

Early in 1911 she was off again — this time for three months in Egypt with the Gardner Cassatts and their family. She joined them in Munich. They missed Athens on account of the quarantine, but intended to return that way. "This is a great change for me," she wrote Minnie. She could hardly believe she was sitting on deck being towed to Luxor. Later when they were cruising down the Nile, the boat struck a sandbar. The two little girls — Ellen Mary Cassatt and her sister, Eugenia — wanted to jump in for a swim in the Nile, but their parents were doubtful. "Nonsense," said Mary. "There are no crocodiles here. Let them." *

Nothing is said about Mary's purchasing special clothes for this trip on the Nile. But when her brother Gardner invited her to go on a Mediterranean cruise in his yacht, she ordered an appropriate wardrobe. The investment turned out to be wasted, however, for just out of Marseille Mary became so violently seasick she had to be put ashore at Genoa.

Elegant but tailored in her choice of clothes, she permitted herself to be extravagant about hats. It was the period of large, often plumed millinery, and she was a happy patron of Reboux of Paris. Otherwise she was as reasonably thrifty about clothes as she was in other matters. In her early days abroad, when her sister wrote her from America requesting a dress from one of the Paris houses, Mary "had a good wear out of

* Mary Cassatt's niece, Mrs. Hare, said, *"This was always her attitude toward children who adored her."*

it" before shipping it across the Atlantic. She was pleased with her foresight when it was lost in transit. Another time, visiting a dressmaker in behalf of Aleck's wife, she saw some of the dresses for an acquaintance's trousseau and was astonished that it included sixty-five dresses and sixty-five pairs of shoes embroidered to match the dresses!

While at Grasse not long before the war, she was intrigued by a letter from Minnie describing her visit to Berlin and Munich. "I had no idea," Mary wrote her, "that Berlin was so amusing . . . . The opera in Munich is much the same as in Berlin as regards the women's dressing. I cannot understand why they don't wear light clothes, if they don't want to be 'décolleté.' It used to [be] so at the theatres in Paris. Now they dress almost as much as for the Opera . . . . I hope you enjoy being presented. The Empress isn't agreeable and 'finds fault with everything,' so I heard this afternoon. It is the men who are decorative in Germany with their uniforms. The Emperor would not allow one of my pictures in the Museum . . . . Mrs. Havemeyer told one of his aides in New York that he knew nothing of art! . . ."

In August 1910 the statue of her brother, Alexander J. Cassatt, was ready for unveiling in the Pennsylvania Station in New York. Mary's nephew Eddie, the elder son, pulled the cord that exposed the statue to view. Writing to his mother, who was away at the time, Eddie said, "It is wonderful how Mr. W. [the sculptor] has caught the sweetness and kindness that always shined through even his most serious and sternest expressions of face." When Mary saw the newspaper pictures of the statue, she wrote Rob: "It seems to me like him. It must be, for someone told me he hadn't to read the name — he recognized it as being my brother from the family likeness to me!

I suppose it is too much to hope it is a work of art but a good likeness is something . . . . It is very comforting to think they recognize your Father's ability and do justice to his character." Then she rapped the knuckles of the American President: "I don't know if Roosevelt will have his statue. I doubt it if he lives long enough, for by that time he will be found out. His progress over here was grotesque. At the Embassy he waited until everyone had arrived and then went the rounds like royalty with a word for everyone. His speech at the Sorbonne amused these clever Frenchmen when they read the translation."

Though her conversation and her letters were as brisk as ever in the years before the war, her health was far from robust. Before long she was overtaken by serious illness. For her slow recovery she went to the south of France and took a little house in Grasse, the Villa Angeletto. "It is small, just enough for me. It has lately been done over and added to, in fact it is not yet finished, but has the modern comforts and now all I want is the sun. The servants, dogs and auto are here and it feels now like home."

They had had a war scare. "No one wants to begin, and it would be an awful war, every nation in Europe engaged. For a time the banks would give no gold, but that is over. Of course I was worried for Mathilde is a German and the first thing would be to expel all Germans. It would make havoc among travelers, for all over France the hotels are all managed and run by Germans."

The day after Christmas, 1911, she wrote to Durand-Ruel from Grasse: "It takes some time to acclimatize oneself here, at least three or four weeks. I could not walk 300 meters upon arriving; now I make a kilometer and a half without too much fatigue" — about five times as far. "I am not working yet. My doctor tells me to take it easy until my energy returns and until I have lost my pains. I am bored with solitude and with idleness, of course." [6] She had seen Degas' nieces and had reported to them that when she had last seen their uncle she had found him very changed.

Two weeks later she had a serious relapse and felt as ill as when she arrived — "I who believed I would be able to work the fifteenth of January!" Then to business regardless of how sick she felt: "I have written to my concierge; when you go to the rue Marignan he has orders to take down the pictures you wish to take away. When you have the two things *chez vous*, tell me what you think of them." She closed the letter, "A thousand good things, dear sir, for you and yours and good health to you — it is the best thing in life." [7]

Ill though she was, the world of art was on her mind. "I am going to write you after the Ronard sale," she told Minnie, "where pictures by Degas, Manet and Monet are to be sold for I want Rob to know the value of the pictures his Father left. I put them down at $200,000 at least. From all over Europe buyers will be in Paris. I ought to be making my fortune, but that is the way things go — here when my pictures are sought for, I cannot work!" Later she had to decide she was not strong enough to run up to Paris to see Minnie. "I feel an itching to take the train, but I know I ought not." Still there was one thing she could do to show her affection. "I can at least be-flower you. This is one of the pleasures here — to send flowers to our friends."

At a later time, when Minnie and Rob were both in France, Mary wrote from Beaufresne that she had had a setback with her sight. The letter in heavy ink was hard to read, but she managed to give Minnie the names of houses where purchases might be made to advantage, furs in one instance, furniture and tapestries in the other. And she was glad Rob had made a trip by plane. "It is an easier way of traveling than over these bumping roads."

George Biddle, at that time a young artist and a fellow-Philadelphian, met Mary Cassatt in 1912, when she was already beginning to lose her sight. "She had influenced my work more than any other artist whom I had known," [8] he recorded in his book. At the time, she was recovering from an illness "brought on in part by the death of her brother, J.G. [Gardner] whom she adored." He said also, "The qualities that made her very great to me were her integrity and her passion. She drew that almost impossible line between her social life and her art, and never sacrificed an iota of either." And again: "She had a veneration for Degas. What he felt was actually her law and standard. Pointing to a little grisaille on her wall she added, 'And no painter since Vermeer has mastered atmosphere the way he does.' That was that. I have never seen a great and successful artist who so ungrudgingly acknowledged the debt to an earlier and lifelong influence, but it was not generosity with Miss Cassatt so much as her splendid detachment." [9]

Toward the end of 1912 Mary wrote Durand-Ruel from Grasse that she wanted him to sell the portrait Degas had made of her. She was anxious that it should not be left to her family as a portrait of herself. "It has qualities of art, but is so distressing and shows me as a person so repugnant that I would not want anyone to know that I posed for it. The picture is framed and there is a glass over it . . . . If you believe my portrait to be saleable, I would like it to be sold to a stranger and especially that my name should not be attached to it." She wanted him to sell also two other Degas belonging to her.

Later she said that if he believed no one would recognize her in the picture, it was all the same to her where the picture was sold. "It seems to me that one might be more apt to find a purchaser in Germany or in France than in America, but I leave that to you." In a postscript: "As for the price of the picture, I leave that to you. I cannot make an estimate of its value — that is a distressing but a very strong feeling. It seems to me a true Degas." [10] About three months later Durand-Ruel informed her that Vollard, the art dealer, had bought the portrait.

While these negotiations were going on, Mary devoted a rainy day to answering an inquiry from her niece, Ellen Mary Cassatt, about the cubists and others: "No Frenchman of any standing in the art world has ever taken any of these things seriously. As to Matisse, one has only to see his early work to understand him. His pictures were extremely feeble in execution and very commonplace in vision. As he is intelligent he saw that real excellence, which would bring him consideration, was not for him on that line. He shut himself up for years and evolved these things; he knew that in the present anarchical state of things — not only in the art world but everywhere — he would achieve notoriety — and he has. At his exhibition in Paris you never hear French spoken, only German, Scandinavian and other Germanic languages; and then people think notoriety is fame and even buy these pictures or daubs. Of course all this has only 'un temps'; it will die out. Only really good work survives."

Mary then wrote with displeasure of the Steins, of Gertrude and of the two brothers who started a studio, "bought Matisse's pictures cheap and began to pose as amateurs of the only real art . . . . the pose was, if you don't admire these daubs I am sorry for you; you are not of the chosen few." Many people

went to their receptions, "but I never would, being too old a
bird to be caught by chaff."

She went on to explain the difference between this period
and the earlier one. "The misunderstanding in art has arisen
from the fact that forty years ago — to be exact, thirty-nine
years ago — when Degas and Monet, Renoir and I first exhibited, the public did not understand, only the 'élite' bought
and time has proved their knowledge. Though the public in
those days did not understand, the artists did . . . . Now the
public say — the foreign public — Degas and the others were
laughed at; well, we will be wiser than they. We will show we
know; not knowing that the art world of those days did accept
these men . . . . No sound artist ever looked except with scorn
at these cubists and Matisse."

During the spring of 1913 Mary expressed her concern to
Durand-Ruel about the behavior of Degas to his nieces. In his
increasing blindness and consequent despair over being unable
to work as he wished, he was making them a butt of his sharp-
tongued fury. Among other things, he insisted they were only
concerned about what they would inherit from him. Mary,
who knew so well the kindness and affection buried deep in
her cantankerous old colleague, was indignant at his behavior.
"His nieces only ask to be devoted to him. Mlle Fèvre is intelligent. I shall advise her to find a pretext for going to Paris,
but her uncle is truly terrible with them and also with his
nephew. He tells them that they are only concerned about
death-duties and other things still more severe. Naturally they
are proud of his great reputation as an artist . . . ." [11]

Early in 1914 Durand-Ruel wrote her about another exhibition of her work, but she felt her pictures had been shown
too much unless she had new work to add. "As for a showing
of Degas' pastels and paintings for the benefit of women's

suffrage, the idea is '*assez piquante*,' if Degas knows about it."
Further, she did not want to sell her picture, *La Barque* (National Gallery of Art, Washington). She had already promised
it to her family. It was made at Antibes twenty years before,
the year that her niece was born. "That year and that make
it a souvenir." She added, "I have so little to leave them, to
my nieces and nephews!" [12]

She also told Durand-Ruel that her friend Mr. Stillman
was at Cannes. He had told her that Ollendorff, the publisher
of Achille Segard's book * about her, "was one of their good
books, meaning because of its sale, I suppose. If that is so,
Mr. Stillman has greatly contributed to it." [13] Soon she wrote
again saying she had not been at all aware that Mr. Stillman
had bought the Segard books. He had not spoken to her about
it, though he had been to see her recently with the Ambassador and his wife.

Just as many of Mary Cassatt's guests were from America, so
her work continued to reflect the country where she was born.
Looking back from 1947, the Wildenstein Gallery noted in
the foreword to the catalogue of their loan exhibition of her
work that she was not only American by birth "but also by
many of the best qualities of her art — spontaneity, natural
freshness, and that deep honesty of expression which is so
characteristic of every American endeavor in art. She succeeded
in preserving these qualities intact in the midst of all the
sophistications of her elected impressionist atmosphere, and
along with the poetic features of her painting." [14]

Mrs. Breeskin in the same catalogue considered her qualities
as the French saw them: "The French critics for the most
part were irked by the many attributes that set her apart from

---

* *Mary Cassatt, Un Peintre des Enfants et des Mères.*

the general French temperament and taste. Her scorn of the pretty and the sentimental, her wholesome simplicity, her stress of character and a certain austerity which seemed to them cold, were unsympathetic to them. Charles Ephrussi said, for instance, that she was afflicted with the 'English Terror,' meaning a lack of the French *abandon*." [15] Elaborating this from the French point of view, Arsène Alexandre wrote after her death: "The feeling of her most captivating compositions never has the Latin abandon and tenderness. Does that mean that her work lacks feeling? If it does, we have failed to express our meaning. But it is enough to have known, in however limited a fashion, the everyday life of France and of the English-speaking countries to understand that in the latter affection carries a dignity, a certain reserve which for us, the demonstrative race, has the appearance of coldness." [16] Mellario also recognized her for the American woman she was: "She is wholly original and belongs to her own race. Her art expresses her nation, young, full of new force; she is without prejudice, vital; although she is familiar with the culture of the old world, there is the freshness of a new nation in her art. Her inspiration is from her own epoch, her own race. She expresses the character of the American people, a people awakening to all that is best in art and eager to possess it in abundance." [17]

These achievements did not, however, come to her without sustained exertion. As the Wildenstein foreword noted: "While belonging so well to her own time, Mary Cassatt continued the tradition of French painters deeply devoted to their profession, mastering their art through the slow, tenacious and patient apprenticeship of daily uninterrupted and hard work. Her social standing and material well-being did not prevent her from hammering the destiny of her art in a way which

Courtesy Mount Holyoke College Art Department
South Hadley, Massachusetts
Gift of Ira Langson, 1961

Woman Reclining

supposedly is reserved for those artists who know the hardships of life." [18]

The quality and aim of her hard work is indicated by Hazan: "... her art never froze into system, and she managed to escape all formulas. It is dominated far more by feeling than by technique, and the majority of her works are motherhood scenes of the most tender affection. She gave this hackneyed mother-and-child theme a new freshness by stripping it of all artifice and literature. Just as the great Impressionists show us landscapes in their everyday lighting, Mary Cassatt shows us mother and child in all their simplicity, when their gestures are not made for the purpose of being seen and reproduced. By participating in this rehabilitation of the acts of everyday life, which was a characteristic of the Impressionist movement in which she felt so much at home, Mary Cassatt made a very personal and important contribution to the body of Impressionist creation." [19]

On the thesis that her art was her own and never "froze into system," Christian Brinton quotes a remark attributed to Degas as he studied one of her pictures: "Ça, c'est de Holbein." Brinton then continues: "She emphasizes form itself rather than the atmospheric ambience in which form is enveloped. Her work betrays none of the extremes of 'pleinairisme' or 'pointillisme' so much in vogue during her day. Notably in her rendering of the perennial appeal of the maternal theme does she reveal that 'golden rightness' which is less impressionist than classic in spirit. Allegri, Parmigiano and the treasures of the Museo di Antichità at Parma were not forgotten. Hers is an art in which mind dominates eye. This is precisely the reverse of Impressionism ...." [20]

During the 1900's before the World War, Mary Cassatt had the satisfaction of knowing her work was being shown more and more widely. In the United States her pictures were included in exhibitions in such cities as Boston, Buffalo, Chicago, Indianapolis, Minneapolis, New York, Pittsburgh, Philadelphia, Portland (Oregon), Providence, St. Louis, Seattle, Toledo, Washington, D. C., and Worcester. Abroad there were showings in Berlin, London, Manchester, Munich, Paris and Rome.

In Philadelphia, however, things were not as she would have liked them to be. Biddle observed with perhaps some hyperbole: "With the intellectual world of Paris sitting at her feet Miss Cassatt still wanted more than anything else recognition from Philadelphia and her family. She was given neither. At one time she had wished to present to the Pennsylvania Academy of Fine Arts two portraits by Courbet. 'I felt it would mean so much to the students to have these two fine examples of French portraiture. I went to Durand-Ruel and asked him the price, telling him I could not pay for them at the time. "That's all right, Miss Cassatt," he said. "I will take some of your work in exchange." And do you know what the Academy had the audacity to write me?' she shouted. 'They thanked me and added that by the way they noticed that the Academy had no examples of my own work and would I send them something, hi! hi! hi! I told them I had been exhibiting for years at the Academy and they had never asked me my prices, although they had funds for buying contemporary American art.' " [21]

Steadily Mary Cassatt's eyes were failing but, as the world reeled toward August 1914, useful work remained to be done. She was seventy, but it was still her great satisfaction to make work the firm core of her day.

Chapter IX

THE WAR

Relatives were with Mary Cassatt in the fateful summer of 1914 — Gardner's wife, Jennie, and her two daughters, Ellen Mary and Eugenia. On the surface, life seemed much as usual. In June Durand-Ruel arranged an exhibition of Mary's work in Paris. In July she wrote to George Biddle, who was in Munich: "We are all here leading the 'simple life,' the girls taking French lessons and long walks and seemingly content to be quiet." [1] In the same letter she told him she could not accept the offer he had transmitted that she exhibit in Chicago. She had already promised to send all her work she still owned — three paintings and one pastel — to a New York exhibition of Degas' work and her own. She explained that most of her pictures were owned abroad. She knew he would understand, and she appreciated his interest.

Though Mary had recognized for some time the possibility of war, the outbreak of hostilities took her and her visiting relatives by surprise. On the evening of the invasion of France, her sister-in-law and the girls took the night train for Brussels to buy wine from their usual wine merchant. They arrived about seven in the morning unaware of the invasion. The wine merchant quickly asked Mrs. Cassatt if she had any gold. Learning she had not, he told her he would get her as much as he could and that she must then go straight home. She did as she was told, and back at Beaufresne immediately reserved passage for America.

During the few days before she and her daughters sailed, word came that since Mathilde was German they should get her to the south of France as quickly as possible. Mary recognized the necessity for doing so, but there was no petrol for such a trip. She wrote at once to Clemenceau for authorization to purchase sufficient fuel, and authorization was given. Then a further complication arose. Pierre, the chauffeur, refused to drive a German anywhere unless the family went with him. So Mary went. Taking Mathilde south proved to have been in vain, however. She was peremptorily ordered back to Germany. The following February, Mary wrote her family, "Mathilde and her sister are across the frontier . . . . Poor Mathilde has lost 30 pounds fretting over our separation."

Before Mrs. Gardner Cassatt and her daughters sailed for the United States in September, Mary left Beaufresne and moved her household to Grasse. The Havemeyers begged her to come live with them, but she thought it her duty to stay in France. "Like Myron Herrick, the only foreign ambassador who refused to leave Paris in 1914 to follow the government to Bordeaux, she was bent on remaining in France during the war of 1914-1918, but she had, alas, to leave her *chateau de Beaufresne* situated in the military zone." [2]

From the Villa Angeletto she wrote to Minnie early in the new year: "I am here with my Swiss chambermaid who has been with me more than three years and knows all the ways of the house. She and a cook from Grasse take care of me and the dogs . . . . Pierre is 'conducting' an auto for naval officers . . . . My gardener is at the front since the first. The oldest aide aged 17 has also been called."

Segard says it had pleased Mary Cassatt over the years "to discipline her independence." [3] In her work she had always had to set her own standards and provide her own goals. Some painters she knew had been kept at work by financial pressures or by social ambitions. She had had money and no desire for more social life than she had. Her ambition had been to attain the peak of self-development as an artist. She had worked hard, and her self-criticism had been severe. She was accustomed to discipline. In her painting she had tolerated no glossing over of difficulties. She had faced problems candidly and objectively. She continued to do so as the war closed around her and as ill health interfered more and more with her work. As far as circumstances permitted she kept her self-reliance and met life with sensible fortitude.

Her attitude during the war was as vigorously belligerent as might have been expected. "When a man thinks he is divinely inspired to govern the world he ought to be in an asylum. The only thing to do with a nation fanatically inspired by the same idea is to beat it out of them." Still she kept a sense of proportion and quoted Schiller to George Biddle "to show how the Germans had changed since the Eighteenth Century." [4]

To Minnie she insisted, "No one who is not here can understand how we live. If we do forget this awful drama for half an hour we are brought back with a jerk. Americans are all working hard to help in picking up the pieces." She spoke of one American who had four ambulances at the front "and has saved hundreds of lives." She reported that in England it was thought that August would see the last of the fighting.

The Map

As the war went on and on, there are brief glimpses of her life in her letters. Evidently she was painting again in 1915 for she wrote Durand-Ruel that she had just had word that Mrs. Havemeyer would arrive at Genoa the twentieth of March. "I had believed the twentieth of April. I do so want to work. I really cannot disarrange myself for more than two days and it is so tiring to travel and to talk all the time. I cannot do it." [5] In New York Durand-Ruel exhibited her work in the spring of 1915 and again in April 1917.

Occasionally she went from Grasse to her apartment in Paris. To Minnie she wrote: "I was so very glad to get your letter and would have answered it before I left Paris but after all my other troubles I had a felon on my right thumb which made writing very difficult and worries me yet as I keep it bound up. — I have had a great deal of trouble with my eyes. Two years ago in October I might have been cured in a week had Dr. —— who has a great reputation seen what ought to have been so easy for him to see. I felt I was losing my sight and Dr. B. operated . . . ." She was back at Grasse to get as well as possible "and let my eyes rest and in a couple of months to return to Paris and get spectacles. Dr. B. promises much but I remember my age and don't look forward but live from day to day. In this sea of misery in which we live an individual case seems of little account. There are ten thousand blind in France. Dr. B—— has as many as twenty wounded people in at once, all with both eyes shot out. — Those who have both leg or arm consider themselves very lucky. — When I think of your boys I wonder will they ever see such a war. Oh, my dear Minnie, the women must be up and doing to prevent such another war or it will be the end of humanity. If only the German women could make a revolution but I am afraid there is no hope there." She added, "It seems that the German Government have hired large hotels all over the country to put the insane in . . . ."

She concluded with longing to see her small nephews. "They are not yet too big to have kisses sent them. Give them two from me." She is also grateful to Minnie herself: "It was too dear and kind of you to offer to come over to me. With submarines still about it is much too dangerous. If only we could see the end of this war! Everyone seems resigned to at least a year, even to eighteen months. Who will be left?"

For a while she was back at Beaufresne. George Biddle writes: "One Sunday I bicycled with Abram Poole to lunch with Mary Cassatt at her chateau at Beaufresne. It was the first week of the Somme offensive. We could hear the artillery gently booming to the north. Miss Cassatt opened a bottle of old Burgundy and served us Philadelphia White Mountain Cake — God knows where she got it." [6]

Also from Beaufresne she wrote to Mr. Whittemore in Connecticut: "I have been long in answering your very kind letter which I received nearly two weeks ago. The reason is that I have been impressing on myself the absurdity of keeping a picture to leave to a nephew or niece, who care nothing for art, and certainly not for my pictures. It is a great pleasure and gratification to me that you like and want to own that particular picture, the *Tondo*, for I have always thought it one of my best. Will you do me a favor? Take the *Tondo*, and keep it for some time. If once you have it on your walls and continue to like it then I will sell it to you. The price is five thousand dollars. I don't want the money now. Later when the period of destruction is over and reconstruction begins it may be useful." [7]

She added: "I came out here day before yesterday. It took me more than two weeks to get all the papers necessary to allow me to come here in my auto as this is in the army zone. To live here without horses and without an auto is to be a prisoner. I am hoping the General at Beauvais will give me permission to use my auto in a strictly limited area. It is all I can ask. — We are within fifty miles of the front and General Joffre's headquarters are at Chantilly I am told, that is thirty miles from here.

"As you say the world is mad just now. Where is the end? The French, as an English Admiral wrote to me, are fighting gloriously and we all of course are sure of the ultimate victory." She regretted not being able to accept his invitation to visit them all in "that lovely mountain home which I saw only in early spring. I feel chained here and have duties I must fulfill." [8]

Meanwhile her old friend Degas had withdrawn almost completely from his friends. Nearly blind, unkempt and miserable with the general deterioration of his aging anatomy, he spent his days walking up and down the boulevards or following funeral processions. To Mrs. Havemeyer Mary exclaimed: "Mercy! what a state he is in! He scarcely knows you, he takes no interest in anything. It is dreadful. With millions of francs still in his studio, they can do him no good; he is consumed with old age." [9] And later: "Poor Degas is always the same. What a world it is! Oh, to get out of it without too much suffering!" [10] Mary did not say that one day when Degas was sick in bed, she went to visit him. It was a cloudy day, and she carried an umbrella. Probably she had fiddled with it as she talked to him and made him even more nervous than he usually was. Anyway he suddenly reached out, grabbed the umbrella, thrust it down beside him beneath the blankets and refused to give it back to her.

On September 27, 1917, Mary wrote to George Biddle:

"Degas died at midnight not knowing his state. His death is a deliverance but I am sad. He was my oldest friend here and the last great artist of the Nineteenth Century. I see no one to replace him." [11]

The funeral service, celebrated at Saint-Jean de Montmartre, reunited such artists and friends as Bartholomé, Alexis and Louis Rouart, Monet, Forain, Raffaëlli, the Durand-Ruels, Vollard and others as well as Mary Cassatt. President Poincaré was represented. "But," writes Lemoisne, "in the midst of the great events of 1917, his death did not have the reverberation that such a personality deserved. It is true that Degas had so exaggerated his retirement that the public, always ungrateful, if it admired more and more his magnificent work, had already almost forgotten the man." [12]

Toward the close of the war, Mary's eyes had failed so much she could not distinguish objects. A letter from her to Durand-Ruel in early February 1918 is not in her handwriting. She reported that the cataract was closing very slowly. "I do not believe they will be able to operate before fall." [13] She now had no means of transportation and so was unable, among other things, to call on her neighbor, Renoir. She was also concerned about her Degas' pictures and a pastel of her own. She dreaded lest some misfortune befall the pictures still in her studio. She had arranged to have them taken down and wrapped. What should she do next? — send her gardener for them and have them brought to the country? Or could Durand-Ruel take care of them for her? In the latter case, would it be safer to have them all put in one packing case? A month later she returned to the subject: "Now as for my pictures of Degas', if they are packed up, I would like to send them to America. Do you think that would be possible?"

Then she said another word about Degas' sculpture: "I have seen M. Renoir who told me there were superb things in wax of which M. Vollard showed him photographs." [14]

During the war, other American cities in addition to those already mentioned exhibited Mary Cassatt's work: Brooklyn, Concord, Dallas, Detroit and San Francisco at the Pan-Pacific International Exposition. Pictures by her were also being added to private collections both in America and abroad.

Chapter X

AFTER THE WAR

After the war, though Mary Cassatt was in her seventies and far from well, she continued to express her concern about the future of Degas' work, especially his sculpture, which was then little known. He had modeled in wax, and she was fearful lest these small masterpieces be lost. They should be cast in bronze both to assure their survival and to permit collectors to value this aspect of his work. She reminded his niece that Degas was then recognized by only a small number of people as a sculptor and begged her to go forward with arrangements for casting. She also asked Durand-Ruel if he could not advise M. René Degas to have the Little Dancer cast.* Mary was not the only person anxious to see Degas' work in bronze. Long before his death Vollard had urged Degas to have this done. "When Vollard suggested that he should have one of his little wax statues cast in bronze he refused and destroyed it. Noticing Vollard's disappointment he said, 'You are thinking of its money value only! But even a hat full of diamonds would not make me as happy as I was to destroy it — for all the pleasure I shall have in remodelling it.' " [1]

* In due course the casts were made. One group of them is at the Metropolitan Museum in New York as part of the H. O. Havemeyer Collection.

Though now in her late seventies, Mary Cassatt's vicarious interests in the wider world did not diminish. Her letters mention the general strike in England; two Americans buying Rembrandts, one of them costing $300,000; places in Paris where a suitable mantelpiece might be found for a Philadelphia home; the moving of Cartier's jewelry firm to New York — "there must be plenty of money somewhere." Nearer at hand her attention was caught by the closing of the button factory near Beaufresne. And she was anticipating her return to her country house — "I fancy there will be much to do this summer." She planned to go from Grasse by motor — "It is or was cheaper last autumn than by train notwithstanding the price of gasoline which is now a Government monopoly."

To her great-nephew Alexander, a freshman at Harvard, she sent a small Greuze for his room. She told his mother she hoped he was enjoying his first term. "I think he will have plenty of spirit. Perhaps it will be more spirit than study. Well, what one learns at college doesn't matter if one makes it up afterwards." She was happy that her niece, Ellen Mary Cassatt, was to be married and hoped to see her and her husband, Horace Hare, at Beaufresne as soon as possible after their marriage. In a dictated letter she told her great-niece, Lois,* in the fall of 1921: "I would like to see the photos, but last May I had an operation upon my best eye. The operation was very successful and the oculist promised that I should paint again but a hidden abscess in an apparently sound tooth caused a violent inflammation and I have not yet recovered from it, nor has the sight of the eye returned." Again she wrote her sister-in-law, Jennie, from Paris saying she must have another operation on her eyes in the spring. "It is the impos-

---

* Mrs. John B. Thayer.

sibility of doing anything that is so wearing on the nerves, to me especially who lived only for my work."

Two or three years later, she gave up her villa at Grasse, put electricity in her apartment, and planned to spend her winters in Paris. She hoped Rob and Minnie would be over in the winter (1924), for she was then eighty. "Time passes very quickly and one wants to see one's own before leaving. One hears such sad stories. I don't think Medicine has made much progress and there is far too much surgery." From Beaufresne in November, while she was waiting for the arrival of various young members of the family who were to be her guests, she wrote to Rob: "One thing is good — I have something to do." The following year she sent Rob two portraits — "They will be interesting when the boys are grandfathers."

In 1924 she gave a series of prints to the Petit-Palais. Arsène Alexandre in an article that spring entitled, "Miss Mary Cassatt, Aquafortiste," congratulated the museum on this additon to its collections, saying the series would be of great value in the teaching of original engraving. When the article was read to her, Mary fully agreed with the author that art in the United States had not only become important but was destined to become more so. With him she went back in memory to the travels she had had to undertake in her young days to study masters not then available in America. She was pleased to hear that M. Alexandre felt it was a little puerile for France to claim her as theirs. "It is better," he wrote, "to consider that she and her work have a reach and a tone too broad and too general to be classified other than simply in the family of the Masters." Speaking of her engraving, the author believed that one could use the term consecrated by Ingres — *probité*. "We recall again the surprise and pleasur-

able excitement that we experienced at the first exhibition of
her colored prints, devoted for the most part to the intimate
life of mother, child, and young girl. Nothing was more precise
than the composition, nothing more light and delicate than
the color which had flowered not *on* that precision but at *the
same time* with it." [2] Hearing this view she might have said,
as Degas had in another connection, There is someone who
feels as I do.

There were visitors from America during her last years.
Forbes Watson reported her pronounced views about art training for young Americans: "In the last talk that I had with
Miss Cassatt before she had given up hope of recovering her
sight, she maintained that although in her youth, owing to
conditions in America, it was necessary to become an expa-
triot in order to carry on the profession of painting, expatri-
otism was not only unnecessary for the American student of
this period — it was detrimental because uprooting." Watson
added: "She had enjoyed in France as great a success as a
sincere artist from the United States could expect . . . . Her
house in Mesnil-Théribus was a retreat of infinite charm and
her apartment in Paris reflected a rare sense of living . . . . Art
was her life . . . . She believed in hard labor. As she grew older
she came more and more to look like a woman who had
worked, and since painting to be at all accomplished, requires
long hours of physical strain, Miss Cassatt not surprisingly had
the appearance of a woman trained to the bone by hard physical effort." And further about his observations on his visit:
". . . there was in her, despite her lack of youth, an eagerness
that made the years drop from her . . . . One couldn't listen to
her, pouring out her ardor and her understanding, without
feeling his conviction in the importance of art to civilization

intensified . . . . She made you share her intense hatred of aesthetic prevarication and compromise." [3]

While there may have been outbursts of bitterness during the long years of her almost complete blindness, Mary Cassatt was resourceful in finding work for herself, and her iron determination kept her head high and her common sense intact. Most of all she did not let people see the effort such fortitude cost her. "There was . . . in Mary Cassatt until her death that kind of serenity and wisdom, of generosity of thought and feeling, which are the true reflections of greatness. There was perhaps the subconscious certitude of the ultimate recognition her art would gain in her native and adopted countries to both of whom her artistic heritage belongs." [4]

In both countries her work was exhibited after the war. In New York Durand-Ruel arranged exhibitions in 1920, 1923 and 1924, and in Paris in March 1924. Her work was also exhibited in Paris exhibitions at the Musée du Luxembourg (1919) and at the Salle du Jeu de Paume (1922). Then in the year before her death occurred an event well described by Brinton: "It signalled her entry through the portals of the Palais du Louvre where Degas had long since so spiritedly, perhaps prophetically, envisioned her. The occasion was the superlative showing of *Cinquante Ans de Peinture Française 1875-1925*, arranged under the auspices of the Government. Mary Cassatt was no longer alone and virtually unknown. Her position in the world of art had been officially recognized. Her companions were Daumier, Courbet, Pissarro, Manet, Cézanne, Monet, Degas, Morisot, Renoir, Gauguin, van Gogh, Henri-Matisse and others in kind. She was amongst her rightful compeers. No American artist save Whistler had attained similar distinction in the field of international aesthetic expression." [5]

Young Woman Sewing (*Femme cousant*)

Young Woman Sewing (Femme cousant) now hangs in the Louvre itself; a *Mother and Child* is in the permanent Impressionist collection in the Jeu de Paume.

Personal pleasure came to Mary Cassatt through the interest of her niece, Ellen Mary Cassatt Hare, in Beaufresne. One autumn, when her writing was almost illegible, she wrote to Jennie from there. "I take a great interest in keeping all going now that I think Ellen will keep the place. It is much to have an object in life." *

George Biddle called on her at Beaufresne a few months before her death. He had been invited for lunch, but she had a relapse the preceding day and telegraphed him not to come. The wire did not reach him and so he lunched alone in her dining room with the mirror overhead. When Mary Cassatt received him in her bedroom after lunch, she blamed her disability on the bitterly cold, wet January weather. "My doctor says that in forty years there has not been such a storm." [6] She would have ordered chicken for him, but had not thought he would come. "She hoped the Château Margot was really good.

---

* For some time Mrs. Hare did live at Beaufresne. Then as it became desirable for her to return to America, she deeded the property to a private organization caring for children in memory of Mary Cassatt's devotion to young people. Near the entrance is this plaque:

Mary Stevenson Cassatt
Artiste Peintre
Née à Pittsburgh U. S. A.
Le 22 mai 1843
Décédée à Beaufresne
Le 14 juin 1926
a habité cette propriété
de 1894 à 1926.
Ce domain a été donné en souvenir
d'elle aux oeuvres du Moulin Vert par
sa nièce, Ellen Mary Cassatt-Hare
Le 9 mai 1961.

It was the last bottle of a case of wine presented to her by her brother J.G., just before his death . . . ." On and on she went, doing most of the talking herself and, ill though she was, the room became charged with her "electric vitality." Mathilde had explained to him when she met him at the gate that several months before, Miss Cassatt had fallen from her bed and since then had not been able to walk alone. But almost daily she was carried to her car, for she still loved to drive. When Mr. Biddle saw she was becoming tired, he said he would see her again. Once more she regretted that the bad weather had prevented her coming down to lunch. "She would motor to Paris as soon as it got a little warmer." [7]

Her guest had gone. She supposed she must stay in bed. How annoying to have had a fall. How annoying this vile rainy weather. Yet how beautiful and sheltered her room. She thought of her room in Philadelphia when she was a young girl, and the rain driving against the windows. A cheerful smile passed over her face. It was good to think of America — Ellen Mary planning to live at Beaufresne for a while; Lois happily married with a home of her own; Rob and Minnie with their family, and Alexander with the Kelso spoons. Good too that she had had the chance to leave America, so barren then of art, for study in the great museums. The lovely feeling of tiredness after hard work. The horses, yes, especially her horses and her griffons. The praise of Degas when her line was right. Her blessed family's visits to her. The lovely hard challenge in her work. The beautiful exhibition of Japanese prints she had seen with Degas. The blessing it was that Degas had gone without being aware he was on the verge of death. All the family portraits she had painted. The forty-year devotion of

Playing Chess

(Drawing by Baumgaertner during the Cassatts' visit to Heidelberg, 1854)
From left to right J. Gardner Cassatt, Robert Kelso Cassatt, Mary Stevenson
Cassatt and their father, Robert Simpson Cassatt.

Mathilde. The wonderful satisfaction when the Havemeyers bought beautiful pictures destined for America.

What was that lying on her foot? She asked Mathilde to hand it to her. Oh, a picture of children with their father playing chess, one a little girl in braids. Children, bless them! She had told a young painter not long ago that woman's vocation in life was to bear children. He had naturally supposed she had meant this as criticism of herself. Had she meant herself? She had had nephews and nieces, great nephews and nieces and many other young friends. There were also the children she had painted — some very round ones, others rather flat as in the prints. Her inner gaze went around the walls of her house — her color prints hung there. She could not see them, but they gave her pleasure. She had done well with them. Again the slight smile and a nod of satisfaction as she remembered she had done well also hiding them from the Germans. Before the German officers took Beaufresne for their headquarters, she had had the prints carried to the woodshed and covered with stove wood and kindling. After the war was over there they were, perfectly safe with only one broken frame among the lot. She thought of Beaufresne, how she had enjoyed it. And her roses. This pouring rain would be good for them. It would saturate the subsoil. The spring would be, as always in the country, so tenuous at first, so fresh. The soft wind on one's face. Then the sturdy growing season. She could already feel the prick of the rose thorns as Mathilde cut the blooms and put them in her hands. And the delicious fragrance. She had been wise to concentrate on roses. She must be sure, before the spring was far advanced, to have the gardener . . .

Spring slipped into summer before she left Beaufresne, in mid-June 1926.

The entire village followed the funeral procession, Vollard tells us.* Mary Cassatt may have seemed sometimes to live to herself, but on this final day it was clear enough that no worthy hand had been extended in vain, no needed sympathy withheld. "None but old Mathilde, her devoted maid, and a few intimates," wrote Vollard, "knew the whole extent of her generosity for Mary Cassatt accompanied her acts of benefi- cence by a dry, almost distant gesture as though she felt shy of doing good.

"In the cemetery after the last prayers, the pastor . . . dis- tributed to those present the roses and carnations strewn upon the coffin, that they might scatter them over the grave. Look- ing at this carpet of brilliant flowers, I fancied Mary Cassatt running to fetch a canvas and brushes."

Though living in France for half a century, attaining there her greatest success, though interred in French soil at Mesnil- Théribus, Mary's identification with her native land never left her. So when her will was read it was only natural the opening words should be: "I, Mary Stevenson Cassatt, having my legal domicile in the city of Philadelphia, state of Penn- sylvania, United States of America . . . ."

* In his Recollections of a Picture Dealer.

BIBLIOGRAPHY

Bazin, Germain: *Impressionist Paintings in the Louvre.* London: Thames and Hudson, 1958. New York: Abrams.

Biddle, George: *An American Artist's Story.* Boston: Little, Brown, 1939.

Breeskin, Adelyn D.: *The Graphic Work of Mary Cassatt.* A Catalogue Raisonné. New York: H. Bittner, 1948.

Breuning, Margaret: *Mary Cassatt.* (Hyperion Press). New York: Duell, 1944.

Cabanne, Pierre: *Edgar Degas.* Paris: Editions Pierre Tisné, 1958.

Comfort, George F.: *Art Museums in America.* Boston: H. O. Houghton, 1870.

Degas Letters, edited by Marcel Guerin. Oxford: Bruno Cassirer, 1947.

Duret, Théodore: *Histoire des Peintres Impressionistes.* Paris: Fleury, 1906.

Faust, Camille: *French Impressionists 1860-1900.* London: Duckworth. New York: E. P. Dutton, 1911.

Havemeyer, Louisine W.: *Sixteen to Sixty, Memoirs of a Collector.* New York: Metropolitan Museum of Art, 1961.

Holber, Arthur: *Treasures of the Metropolitan Museum in New York.* New York: R. H. Russell, 1899.

Isham, Samuel: *The History of American Painting.* New York: Macmillan, 1942.

Lake, Carlton, and Maillard, Roger, Editors: *Dictionary of Modern Painting.* Paris: Fernand Hazan. New York: Tudor, 1953, 1964.

Lemoisne, P. A.: *Degas et Son Oeuvre,* 4 vols. Paul Brame et C. M. de Hauke. Paris: Arts et Metiers Graphiques, 1946-1949.

Mack, Gerstie: *Gustave Courbet.* New York: Knopf, 1951.

Mondor, Henri: *Vie de Mallarmé*. Paris: Gallimard, 1946.

Moore, George: *Modern Painting*. London: W. Scott, 1893.

  Reminiscences of the Impressionist Painters. Dublin: Maunsel, 1906.

Perruchot, Henri: *Manet*. Cleveland and New York: World, 1962.

Pissarro, Camille Jacob: *Letters to his Son, Lucien*. Edited with the assistance of Lucien Pissarro by John Rewald. New York: Pantheon, 1943.

Renoir, Jean: *Renoir, My Father*. Boston: Little, Brown, 1958.

Rewald, John: *Pissarro*. New York: Abrams, 1963.

  The History of Impressionism. New York: The Museum of Modern Art, 1961.

Ross, Ishbel: *Silhouette in Diamonds, The Life of Mrs. Potter Palmer*. New York: Harper, 1960.

Rouart, D.: *Correspondence de Berthe Morisot*. Paris: 1950.

Saarinen, Aline B.: *The Proud Possessors*. New York: Random House, 1958.

Segard, Achille: *Mary Cassatt, Un Peintre des Enfants et des Mères*. Paris: Société d'Editions Littéraires et Artistiques. Librairie Paul Ollendorff, 1913.

Sweet, Frederick A.: *Sargent, Whistler and Mary Cassatt*. The Art Institute of Chicago, 1954.

Valerio, Edith: *Mary Cassatt*. Collection "Les Artistes Nouveaux." Paris: Les Editions G. Crès et Cie., 1930.

Venturi, Lionello: *Les Archives de l'Impressionisme*. Vol. II, Letters from Mary Cassatt to Durand-Ruel. Paris, Durand-Ruel, Editeurs, 1939.

Vollard, Ambroise: *En Écoutant Cézanne, Degas, Renoir*. Paris: Grasset, 1938.

  Recollections of a Picture Dealer. London: Constable, 1936.

Watson, Forbes: *Mary Cassatt*. American Artists Series. New York: Whitney Museum of American Art, 1932.

(*Note:* Additional material of interest is included in the references that follow.)

REFERENCES

Headnote: When references are to books listed in the Bibliography, identification is made by the name of the author or compiler.

CHAPTER I

1 Segard, p. 2.
2 *ibid*, p. 4.
3 *ibid*, p. 6.
4 *Masterpieces of European Painting in America* edited by Hans Tietze, Oxford University Press, N. Y., 1939.
5 *ibid*.
6 Segard, p. 6.
7 A *Glance in Retrospect* by Christian Brinton in the catalogue of The Mary Cassatt Exhibition, Haverford College, 1939.
8 Segard, p. 7.
9 *Pennsylvania Museum Bulletin*, Vol. 22, pp. 373-382.
10 Segard, p. 7.
11 *ibid*, p. 35.
12 Brinton, *supra*.
13 Renoir, p. 253.
14 *L'Impressionnists, Journal d'Art*, April 6-28, 1877, reprinted in Cabanne, p. 92.
15 Lemoisne, Vol. I, p. 191.
16 Segard, pp. 7 and 8.
17 *Philadelphia Pays Tribute to Mary Cassatt* by Forbes Watson, *Arts*, June, 1927.

18 *ibid.*
19 Segard, pp. 17, 19, 20, 23, 24.
20 *The History of Impressionism* by John Rewald, p. 85.
21 Havemeyer Memoirs, p. 226.
22 *Reminiscences of the Impressionist Painters* by George Moore, pp. 26 and 28.
23 *ibid*, pp. 29 and 30.
24 Segard, p. 45.
25 Pissarro's Letters, p. 216.
26 Segard, pp. 21 and 22.
27 Rewald, *The History of Impressionism,* p. 220 quoting P. Burty as quoted by C. Roger-Marx: *Maîtres d'hier et d'aujourd'hui,* Paris, 1914.
28 *French XVIII Century Painters,* by E. and J. de Goncourt, London, 1948, Phaidon Press, p. 259.
29 Faust, p. 142, *et seq.*
30 Rewald, *The History of Impressionism,* p. 292.
31 Rouart, p. 111.
32 *ibid*, p. 116.
33 Venturi, I, pp. 17, 18.

CHAPTER II

1 *L'Art Moderne,* Paris 1883, pp. 6 and 7.
2 *ibid*, p. 6.
3 Degas Letters, pp. 50 and 51.
4 *ibid*, p. 54.
5 *ibid*, p. 52.
6 Quoted by Adelyn D. Breeskin in the Wildenstein Catalogue of the Mary Cassatt exhibition 1947, p. 20.
7 Degas Letters, p. 6.
8 *ibid*, pp. 171 and 172.
9 Preface to the *Hommage à Mary Cassatt* exhibition at Beaufresne and in Beauvais June-July 1965, by Yvon Bizardel, Directeur Honoraire des Beaux-Arts de Paris.
10 Cabanne, p. 6.
11 *ibid*, p. 83.

12   December 5, 1872.
13   Cabanne, p. 26.
14   *ibid*, p. 36.
15   *ibid*, p. 77 quoting in italics John Rewald, *Histoire de l'Impressionnisme*, Paris: Albin-Michel, 1955, p. 247.
16   *The Degas-Cassatt Story* by T.B.H., *Art News*, Vol. 46, p. 53, Nov. 1947.
17   Havemeyer Memoirs, pp. 244 and 245.
18   André Mellario in *L'Art et Les Artistes*, Nov. 1910.
19   Degas Letters, pp. 55 and 56.
20   *Le Figaro*, April 10, 1881.
21   Pissarro's Letters, p. 23.
22   Havemeyer Memoirs, p. 190.
23   Barbara N. Parker quoted in *Art Digest*, Vol. 17, p. 7, Oct. 1, 1942.
24   *The Art News*, Vol. 36, p. 20, May 28, 1938.
25   Frederick A. Sweet in the catalogue *Sargent, Whistler and Mary Cassatt*, The Art Institute of Chicago, 1954.
26   Pissarro: *Letters à son Fils Lucien*, Paris, 1950. Letter dated May 11, 1883 as quoted by Rewald, *The History of Impressionism*, p. 482 and note 5, p. 519.
27   Rewald, *The History of Impressionism*, p. 484.
28   *ibid*, p. 476.
29   *New York World Telegram*, Nov. 4, 1939.

CHAPTER III

1   Degas Letters, p. 130.
2   *ibid*, p. 125.
3   Havemeyer Memoirs.
4   Mary Cassatt to Mr. Whittemore.
5   Rewald, *The History of Impressionism*, p. 521.
6   Pissarro's Letters, pp. 73 and 74.
7   Rewald, *supra*, 522.
8   Pissarro's Letters, p. 71.
9   *ibid*.
10   Degas Letters, p. 81.

11 *Renoir, My Father* by Jean Renoir, Little Brown, Boston, 1958, pp. 253 and 254.
12 *The New York Herald*, April 10, 1886.
13 *The New York Daily Tribune*, April 10, 1886.
14 *The New York Times*, May 28, 1886.
15 *The New York World*, May 29, 1886.
16 *The New York Herald*, May 25, 1886.
17 Rewald, *The History of Impressionism*, p. 531.
18 Bazin, p. 66.
19 Segard, p. 44.
20 Isham, p. 412.
21 Segard, pp. 50 and 51.
22 *ibid*, pp. 55-57.

CHAPTER IV

1   *L'Art Dans Deux Mondes*, November 19, 1890, p. 7.
2   *ibid*, p. 3.
3   *ibid*.
4   To Mrs. Potter Palmer, Oct. 11.
5   *Mary Cassatt, Sa Vie, Son Oeuvre* by Simone Cammas, Conservateur du Musée Départmental de l'Oise, Beauvais in the catalogue, *Hommage à Mary Cassatt*, June-July 1965.
6   Breeskin, pp. 20 and 26.
7   Lemoisne, Vol. I, p. 192.
8   *Mary Cassatt: American Component in Impressionism* by Jerome Mellquist, *Apollo*, Vol. 71, p. 124, April 1960.
9   Edith Hoffman in *Burlington Magazine*, Vol. 100, p. 454, December 1958.
10 Kathleen Morand in *Burlington Magazine*, Vol. 102, p. 44, January 1960.
11 Segard, p. 109.
12 *American Magazine of Art*, Vol. 42, p. 35, January 1949.
13 O'Connor in The Carnegie Institute's magazine, Vol. 23, p. 134, November 1949.
14 Segard, p. 104.
15 *ibid*.

16 Lemoisne, Vol. I, pp. 192 and 193.

17 Metropolitan Museum of Art, Bulletin n.s.l.: opp. 236, March 1943.

18 Allen S. Weller, *Art Digest*, Vol. 28, p. 6 *et seq.*, January 15, 1954.

19 *Time*, Vol. 62, p. 92, October 12, 1953.

20 Edgar P. Richardson in *Art News*, Vol. 53, pp. 21-23, April 1954.

21 Degas Letters, p. 117.

22 *ibid*, p. 19.

23 *ibid*, p. 22.

24 *Modern Painting* by George Moore.

25 Allen S. Weller, *Art Digest*, Vol. 28, p. 6, January 15, 1954.

26 Segard, p. 26.

27 Degas Letters, p. 144.

CHAPTER V

1 Pissarro's Letters, Nov. 20, 1883.

2 Venturi, Vol. II. Letter of Febr. 18, 1892.

3 To Miss Hallowell from Mary Cassatt, undated.

4 To Mrs. Potter Palmer from Mary Cassatt, Sept. 10 (1892).

5 To Mrs. MacMonnies from Mary Cassatt from Bachivillers.

6 To Mrs. Potter Palmer from Mary Cassatt, Oct. 11.

7 *ibid*, Dec. 1.

8 Pissarro's Letters, p. 222, Nov. 27, 1893.

9 To Mr. Whittemore from Mary Cassatt, February from Cap d' Antibes.

10 Pissarro's Letters, Nov. 27, 1893, p. 222.

11 *ibid*, p. 244.

12 *ibid*, p. 240.

13 *ibid*, p. 319.

14 Degas Letters, p. 195.

15 *ibid*, pp. 197 and 199.

16 To Mrs. Pope from Mary Cassatt, April 7 (1900).

CHAPTER VI

1 Forbes Watson.
2 Havemeyer Memoirs, pp. 249 and 250.
3 Venturi, Vol. II, pp. 114-138.
4 Havemeyer Memoirs, p. 158.
5 *ibid*, p. 154.
6 *ibid*, p. 155.

CHAPTER VII

1 *The Christian Science Monitor*, Boston, Nov. 4, 1932.
2 *Recalling Mary Cassatt* by Helen W. Henderson, *Phila. Inquirer-Public Ledger*, March 10, 1935.
3 *Mary Cassatt* by Adelyn D. Breeskin, The Wildenstein Catalogue for the 1947 Loan Exhibition, New York.
4 *Some Memories of Mary Cassatt* by George Biddle, *The Arts*, Vol. 10, July-Dec., 1926.
5 Camille Mauclair: *Un Peintre de l'Enfance, Miss Mary Cassatt* in *L'Art Decoratif*, Aug. 1902.
6 Biddle, p. 219.
7 Havemeyer Memoirs, pp. 229-231.
8 *ibid*, pp. 234 and 235.
9 *ibid*, p. 251.
10 *ibid*, pp. 251 *et seq.*
11 *ibid*, pp. 252 and 253.
12 *ibid*, pp. 255 and 256; p. 245.
13 *ibid*, p. 264.
14 Dec. 4 (1904?) to Mr. French.
15 To Mrs. Beame from Mary Cassatt, Oct. 19.
16 Venturi, Vol. II, Nov. 10, 1905.
17 *ibid*, Nov. 1905.
18 Vollard, pp. 180 and 181.
19 Private information.

CHAPTER VIII

1 Private information.
2 Renoir, p. 253.
3 Forbes Watson.
4 Catalogue of the Haverford Exhibition, p. 5.
5 Venturi, Vol. II, May 21, 1910.
6 *ibid*, 1911.
7 *ibid*, Jan. 8, 1912.
8 Biddle, p. 217.
9 *ibid*, p. 222.
10 Venturi, Vol. II, pp. 129 and 130.
11 *ibid*, p. 131.
12 *ibid*, Febr. 12, 1914.
13 *ibid*.
14 Foreword, signed "G.W."
15 *Mary Cassatt* by Adelyn D. Breeskin, *supra*.
16 *La Collection Havemeyer et Miss Cassatt* by Arsène Alexander, *La Renaissance*, Febr. 1930.
17 Mellerio.
18 Foreword signed "G.W."
19 Lake and Maillard.
20 Haverford Catalogue, *supra*.
21 Biddle, pp. 222 and 223.

CHAPTER IX

1 National Archives, Washington, D. C.
2 *Preface* to the catalogue for the exhibition, *Hommage à Mary Cassatt* held at Beaufresne and Beauvais, by Yvon Bizardel, Directeur Honoraire des Beaux-Arts de Paris.
3 Segard, p. 33.
4 Biddle, p. 225.
5 Venturi, Vol. II, Febr. 17, 1915.
6 Biddle, p. 150.
7 Mary Cassatt to Mr. Whittemore.

8   *ibid.*
9   Havemeyer Memoirs, p. 249.
10   *ibid*, p. 267.
11   National Archives, Washington, D. C.
12   Lemoisne, Vol. I, p. 202.
13   Venturi, Vol. II, Febr. 9, 1918.
14   *ibid*, March 13, 1918.

CHAPTER X

1   Degas Letters, Annotations, p. 265.
2   *La Renaissance de l'Art Français et des Industries de Luxe,*
    March 1924.
3   Watson.
4   Foreword to the Wildenstein Catalogue, *supra.*
5   A *Glance in Retrospect, supra.*
6   Biddle, p. 219.
7   *ibid*, p. 220.

INDEX